Non Compass Mentis

by
John Fengler

Copyright © John Fengler 2023

All rights reserved

ISBN
Paperback version
9798861198295
Hardback version
9798864189009

No part of this publication may be reproduced, distributed, or transmitted in any form or by any means, including photocopying, recording, or other electronic or mechanical methods, without the prior written permission of the publisher, except as permitted by U.S. copyright law.

For permission requests please contact -

John Fengler at Fenglerauthor@gmail.com

***

With love and affection for

Paul Dorsey for his praise, encouragement, his love of whiskey sours, and who once described me as the "best writer in Southeast Asia who hasn't written a book" -and who left the party way too soon.

Alastair McCloud for his inspiration, wit and use of reverse psychology, who got this ball rolling.

Matt Carrell for his love, albeit tough at times, great friendship, editing and publishing prowess and for not giving me a bill… yet.

Kevin S. Cummings for being a constant champion, sounding board and the first to ever put me in print.

Eoin Donnelly for his relentless badgering and his cash filled envelopes.

To the Chiang Mai writer's group who said;
"Yeah, your grammar, punctuation and spelling are shit, but you've got voice, keep going.

To the wonderfully eclectic gang at Check Inn 99 who welcomed strays a long time ago.

And to my legion of wonderful friends who for as long as I can remember have been telling me to "put 'em in a book".

***

Manywhere

I asked an old Thai girlfriend about her travels, if she'd ever been anywhere. She enthusiastically responded with;
"Oh, I been manywhere".
To date it was the most fabulous and descriptive word that doesn't exist but should that I've ever heard.

I too have been manywhere, be it foreign travels far from shore, or riding around all day in an ambulance in a city full of immigrants. Every hour is another stamp in your passport, each tenement, mansion, alley, rail yard, shelter is a visit to a culture, a time and a place you'd most likely not be welcomed to on a day off in civilian clothes. It was a privilege not afforded to many, for which I am eternally grateful.

John Fengler

***

Originally from New York, John has lived and worked extensively in San Francisco and Southeast Asia and worked in film, emergency medicine and politics.
He currently splits his time between Thailand and Cambodia.

***

Occam's Razor

A friend of mine had posted from the stunning beachfront 'screensaver' vista of Prechuap Khiri Khan in southern Thailand, which made me remember a breakfast there a few years ago.

Eating my muesli at a random coastal guesthouse while observing a gaunt and withdrawn chain-smoker at the next table hand-rolling cigarette after cigarette, while quietly scanning the rooftops and alleys, and actively avoiding eye contact with me. A man full of angst, despair, fear and confusion.

If this had been in a cafe in San Francisco I would have thought of a man whose fifteen-year marriage had gone awry, or someone with their thirty-fourth week on the dole approaching and no financial relief in sight. A man whose diagnosis, just reconfirmed by a fourth specialist, means it doesn't really matter where he spends the next three to six months after all. A man whose wife and daughter he had finally been able to get visas for, after five years of trying, arriving only to have them rejected and sent back to Iraq because of the political caprice of the day. But here, I imagine he's a French journalist fresh from some frontline atrocity in Kurdistan that he witnessed and was intimidated into not reporting. I see a man who feels the Interpol net closing in on him, which in some ways would be preferable to the Chechen mobsters who don't care that it wasn't his fault that the last shipment was stolen. He is a man whose last eighteen months as a black site interrogator in the Philippines has left him broken, his moral compass shattered in so many pieces, hanging out in a beach town with nothing higher than a two-story building around should his demons get the better of him again.

And as the sober light of day and a third cup of coffee takes hold of me, Occam's razor suggests that it's just a hangover from a Thai New Year's Eve party last night being witnessed by a nosy neighbor.

***

A Fork in the Road
Dateline: Khun Sa's Golden Triangle, 1982.

I was traveling with my good friend Claude; a tall, lanky, hilarious, woolen skullcap-wearing Frenchman. We were standing on the banks of the Mekong, looking at forbidden Laos and not-recommended Burma. Burma was closer. We both winked at each other and stripped. I'd never seen him without his woolen hat. He shyly responded to my unasked question;
"Is because I 'ave no 'air."
"How did you lose it?"
"You know I 'ave no idea. Jus' one day I wake up and is gone."
You know you never told me what you did back home by the way. You know, for a living?
"Oh I work in… I am clean out ze water tank in ze, how you say, nuclear reactor."
"Really?! And it just fell out one day, huh??"

Naked under the broiling Thai sun we dove into the Mekong, playfully racing each other to the nearest shore.
Ha! Burma!
Mid high-five we catch movement from the brush as a phalanx of Burmese military emerge 'en garde' from the jungle foliage. Not the first nor the last time to have an AK-47 nervously pointed at me, but it keeps you fresh for sure. An understandably humorless captain stepped forward and presumably started to ask for our passports, then reassessed our resources. We both offered weak smiles and upturned hands. We were naked! In Burma! With a military patrol. No papers, no excuses.
The captain clearly flummoxed, took his pistol and flipped it towards the Thai shore from which we had just come.

We nodded our apologies and appreciation and... well, I don't remember the actual swim. It was my Jesus moment, walking on water. Another high five as we donned our shorts and t-shirts and returned to our fifty-cent a night thatched roof bungalow.

Our story spread amongst the now drunken teenage Thai military patrol that was our stronghold, and we curried great favor. One of the leaders called me over to share in their meal. He leaned on his rifle and gestured me towards a bowl of something that looked like raw pork. I said;

"What is it?"

"Oh... is raw pork. You eat!!"

"Um hhmm, you're drunk, well-armed and we're a thousand miles from a real hospital, yeah sure."

The next morning, I woke up *'mai sabai'*, that is, not feeling my best. Not since the peyote days of yore did I vomit so much. My travel companion Claude said;

"Well zis is too much puke and shit for me, I go travel for a few days and see you after you are better."

Really, I did love the guy.

For the next year or so...OK maybe it was a day or two, hard to say, I lay writhing on a bamboo floor, returning all my precious bodily fluids to the earth. At some point a couple of days into this, a *pakowma* (a kind of Thai sarong) wearing man, who I had seen earlier in the week wearing a military uniform, came by to collect his $1.50 for the three days overdue rent. He saw me laying on the floor and said;

"Oh, OK, OK", and then left.

He returned sometime later with a piece of brown paper that was coated with a thick brown paste. He smiled and mimed a licking motion for me then handed me the paper. It was bitter but, I didn't want to seem unappreciative, and hell I was hallucinating at that point anyway.

Best damn stuff I've ever had. Pain gone, chills gone, vomiting, not that there was anything left, gone.

The Golden Triangle was shining its amber light upon me. To quote Bill Maher; "Ya know I don't do heroin, I don't advocate it's use, hell I wouldn't even know where to get any... but it hasn't hurt my record collection any!"

Raw opium. Well, I have no complaints.

A couple of days later I was good to go.

My landlord/ 'dealer' had returned to his military border police duties and invited me out on patrol with him. We were going upriver into Shan state to deliver 'medicines' to a Karen village. He slung his AK-47 over his shoulder and powered up the longtail boat. We hit the shore a while later, the very same side I'd been chased from days earlier. The nuances of the autonomous state's relationships remain a mystery to me to this day, but there was an alert nonchalance in my guide's demeanor that was comforting to me. I felt more like the guns that everyone wore, were more like the *jambia*, the ceremonial knives carried by wealthy Yemenis, or the scabbards carried by Sikhs, a kind of religious icon, more than anything intended for combat. Wishful thinking perhaps?

We hiked a bit through well-worn jungle paths, until coming to a collection of bamboo homes. It seemed they were no strangers to seeing shiny white faces there, even ones that weren't carrying 'the good book'. I was welcome. We were ushered into one home by a local soldier, and a quick exchange of goods between my military guide and what I took to be the mayor of the village ensued amongst wary glances.

Medicines -yeah, that's what they were!

Transaction complete I was motioned to sit on a rickety chair made of thatch. A teenage Karen hilltribe girl then emerged from a separate kitchen area, carrying a tray with a couple of ceramic cups and a tea pot on it.

She was wearing a t-shirt that displayed a large picture of Sylvester the cat, which incredibly and improbably had written underneath it,

"Happiness is a warm pussy."

The translation, implications, and irony seemed thankfully lost on all, especially the wearer, who was just happy to have a cartoon souvenir from her former Christian missionary educators. It was just some more of the flotsam and jetsam from the outside world that wound up in unlikely places, like the Chadian rebels who wound up with a case of pre-printed 'Pittsburgh Steelers World Super Bowl Champions' jerseys in 2011. They lost that year.

Eventually we returned whence we came, and the next day I finally took my leave. I set off on a solo trek. It was the days before organized eco-tours, when Lonely Planet lived up to its name. I was out about an hour, on a dusty road to some hilltribe village where I was told you could share a pipe with the elders. I came to a crossroads. If you had seen this in a movie, you would have said 'bullshit', but there was an old man sitting right at the 'Y'. I asked him if the road to the right went to the village I was looking for. He smiled and said;

"Yes".

I thanked him and headed down the road. I got about a hundred yards and stopped. I thought;

"Hhmm, I've been in Thailand long enough and…"

So, I returned to the crossroads and said;

"Say, does the road to the left go to the village?"

Sure enough he smiled and said;

"Yes".

My first important Thai lesson in truth-telling was; both roads did indeed lead to where I was going, except the road to the left took about an hour, and the road to the right took about a month.

He wasn't lyin'. But he sure wasn't telling the truth.

***

The Elders

In 2013 I was passing through Rangoon (just not down with the new name) on my way to Rakhine state and stopped into the iconic Strand Hotel for a drink. I was politely stopped by U.S, Secret Service.

"Excuse me sir, may I ask you to wait in the bar for a little while?"

"Actually, it's where I was heading. Why?"

"The Elders are returning to the hotel now, and for security reasons, we need to clear the lobby."

"Elders?"

"Jimmy Carter and Kofi Annan."

Not even a glimpse, sorry to say, but thrilling nonetheless.

Seven hours up the Salween River; Sittwe to Mrauk U, Rakhine State, Burma, 2013… After a long afternoon, touring temples, intermittently being cat-called and pelted with rocks by Arakan locals who mistook me for a Rohingya sympathizing aid worker, I ducked into a market.

Some guy spooked up behind me and barked;

"Hey, who are you?"

"Huh, oh, hi there. Who are you?"

"There are only seventy-five westerners registered to be in this part of the country, and you're not one of them."

"How do you know?"

"It's my job to know."

"Well, I'm just a wayward traveler."

"Well Mr... Wayward Traveler... curfew is in twenty minutes and military patrols will be on the road shortly after. You'd best get back to wherever you're staying."

"I'm not worried."

"Ya should be. Cheers."

Remanded to the post-curfew, one channel TV in my hotel room, a Korean movie with Burmese subtitles. It was about the mid-life crisis of a women's volleyball team coach who was trying to come to terms with his own mediocrity, despite his relentless efforts towards perfectionism.

Either that or it was about a grocery clerk's infatuation with a super model who shopped in his store every day, who was in turn dealing with her own failings in life.

Or it was about a guy in a loveless marriage trying to make ends meet and deciding whether to feed the family with their pet dog.

I had no idea what it was about.

***

The Three Blackbirds

I had a friend in San Francisco a few decades ago, who offered English lessons to rich European girls on holiday who wanted a high society full immersion cultural experience. It was a glorified gigolo service. For a single guy it was utopia. He called me up one day and said he had;

"Just too many of 'em, man. Can you help me out tonight? You'll be comp'd on everything!"

Hhmmm, seventeen beautiful, young Spanish, Polish, German and Italian girls want to go wining, dining and clubbing with two local guys, on their tab?

"Um, OK".

One day turned into several, which turned into one lovely Milanese gal becoming the cream in my coffee. She announced at the would-be end of her trip;

"Oh, I tell my papa to send more money from Milan and I stay with you for two more weeks, OK?"

She even had a pet nickname for me which I loved despite having no real understanding of its meaning, other than taking it as an endearment. I was in love with the idea of having an Italian girlfriend who referred to me in her language. For the initial few weeks we were together I would tell all who met us that I was now to be called; '*Stronzo*.' I was so proud until an Italian speaking friend of mine asked me if I knew what it meant?

He said;

"You know is not so nice. You tell people you are an asshole."

Never one to leave well enough alone I suggested we;

"Keep this thing going. I'll fly to Milan once a month, you fly to New York once a month. It's been done before."

"But you live in California?!"

"We'll meet in New York. It's essentially halfway... come on let's give it a go."

And a month later we met in NY. I had finagled a friend's apartment on the Upper West Side for the week. As soon as she stepped into the apartment a profound and palpable awkwardness settled upon us both. So much so that she had barely put her bags down when I said;

"Hey, let's go out", much to everyone's relief.

There was no hurried loss of clothes, no rush to embrace, no zeal to re-kindle. There was a mutual sense of 'this doesn't feel right, what have we done?' I was hoping those feelings would be short-lived.

We went down to Tribeca, which was in its formative days, before DeNiro had transformed it into the Cannes of New York. They still had loft apartments with monthly rents that were not much more than the tab of a night out at one of the new fancy dinner venues. She'd never been there but suggested a restaurant called *'I Tre Merli'*, The Three Blackbirds.

"My brother's friends have a small place. They are from my hometown. We go visit them, no?"

"Sure."

We arrived at a luxury glass front restaurant which was packed to the gills and had two tuxedoed Italian sentries guarding the doors. They closed ranks as I tried to blaze past.

"You have reservation, sir?"

"Um no, but we'd like to have dinner."

They dismissively laughed, informing us of the several week waiting list. I turned to my fling and said;

"Some little place I know in Tribeca, huh?"

She pushed past me and reached up close to one of the male model guards and softly spoke to him in a local Italian dialect. All the blood drained from the guy's face, and he obsequiously said;

"I'll be right back."

A minute later a grand Fabio-esque man came out, threw his arms around my fling and jovially barked something to the staff just inside. It was a two-floor restaurant with the second floor recessed.

The balcony hung midway over the main downstairs dining area much the way a theatre or opera house is designed.

Four waiters emerged from the wings, one carrying a round table, two others carrying chairs and the last holding a champagne ice bucket and stand. They deftly and apologetically pushed two encroaching tables full of diners back enough to create a space for us at the tip of the balcony. All eyes were upon us, and I imagined the diners were thinking;

"Wow, who the hell is that couple?"

I was wondering the very same thing.

The owner graciously introduced himself to me, let me know that everything tonight was on him and that I should "just enjoy".

He brought a bottle of Absolut which was plunged into the silver ice bucket. A waiter then brought a tray of paper-thin lemon slices with rind, half-covered with espresso grind and half with sugar. He said this was the way to drink vodka in his town. An ice cold shot of Absolut and then a mouthful of sugared coffee and lemon.

The stares continued but lessened in intensity, dulled perhaps by the stimulant effects of the shots. My fling set her carpet bag, which was all the fashion rage back then, down next to the table, threw off her scarf and removed her gloves. All the better to gesticulate with. I asked her once if she sat on her hands would she be able to speak? She laughed and said, "probably no".

We ate a few antipasti which arrived without having been ordered, and then about fifteen minutes in she said;

"I go speak Italian with my friends for a little while, OK? You stay and enjoy."

I owned the world right then, alone at my magic table and my champagne ice bucket on the balcony. Somehow another bottle of Absolut arrived before I realized it had been some time since my fling had left. I chalked it up to 'an Italian thing' and continued ordering items from the menu.

I had a summer job in New York City when I was a teen at an antique center. I remember my boss telling me that whenever gypsies would come in, that I should never watch or follow them. I asked why? He said;

"Because that's when they'll steal!"

That never left me. A gypsy woman happened by my table up on my dining promontory, paused for a moment and left. I studiously avoided looking at her out of a briefly learned habit but did reflexively check for my wallet.

An hour had passed, and then an hour and a half. I didn't know what the rules of time were for friends re-uniting with friends and family from another land, or what my hold or expectations could be with an extended fling, but close to two hours later I decided to go downstairs and check in. They were in the thick of drunken storytelling and all took a moment's pause to try and figure out who the hell I was. My fling was the first to recognize me, albeit with some effort.

She was leaning on one of the male model guards laughing raucously. She then innocently turned to me and said;

"Oh John, I go sleep with this boy tonight, OK? You don't mind? I see you tomorrow, OK?"

She had just flown in that day.

I was stunned. She turned her back to me and continued with the boys. I slinked off to lick my inebriated wounds on the uptown subway.

I got a call from her about noon on the next day asking if I'd taken her carpet bag with me as it had her "passport and everything".

And then the gypsy pause from the night before made sense.

She said she would stay with the boy a few more days, but that we could get together before she left. She offered no further explanation or apology or any seeming acknowledgment of the tacit agreement that had brought us together in this new land.

I gave her the name of the doorman who had her suitcases. The fling had flung.

I never saw her or her carpet bag again.

***

The Bagman

Eating a burger, chatting about John Belushi...and then cocaine became the topic of the day. Forty years later, someone's half eaten and forgotten burrito next to my seat triggered a memory.

A blustery winter's day, late seventies in mid-town Manhattan. Ducked into a Greek diner for a bowl of avgolemono soup. Spotted an empty booth and slid in. And there next to the jar of sugar, the tin of day-old cream and the napkin dispenser was a brown paper bag. Waitresses were buzzing about, calling in orders to the short-order cook, diners were absorbed with their grilled cheese sandwiches, and no one it seemed had noticed the brown paper bag on my table.

I hung back for a few seconds, hands at my sides before sensing the coast to be clear. I pulled the bag to my side of the table, thereby giving me 'legitimate' purchase of its contents without raising suspicion, expecting to see a half-eaten bagel but intuitively knowing it wouldn't be.

I unrolled the top, peered in and saw maybe a hundred thousand dollars' worth of cocaine in a plastic bag. This was New York City in the late seventies. It was boom times on the street and not out of the ordinary to cross paths with cartel contraband.

In a diner in a paper bag though - yeah, a little bit. My mind raced.

Do I snatch it and run and make a windfall, or don't snatch it and run, avoiding a DEA sting, or order my soup and decide later? Just then the front door blasted open, and the sweaty face of a gangster thrust itself in. He was by my booth in an instant. He locked eyes with me and gave a look that was a mix of terror and lethal force.

I immediately dropped my hands to my side, pushed myself upright against the booth back and gave the slightest of nods, letting him know that I was no threat and was just here for the soup… you pathetic loser who forgot his bag of dope.

He glanced down to the formica table and snatched his bounty, holding his glare until he was confident that our business was concluded. No harm, no foul. From start to finish this entire event took less than a minute. A New York minute.

***

The 4th wall

It was about a year after JFK had been assassinated, when my dad took me to see a production of Peter and the Wolf on the Upper West Side of New York. I was seven and still not divested of that certain protective innocence that keeps children's minds safe when the covers are pulled overhead. But at the same time I knew it was just a play. It was just for show.

Peter had already left the gate open. The duck had already gone for a swim, the cat had gone up the tree, and the terrifying wolf was running about the stage trying to catch everyone. I was crammed as far into my center-aisle seat as I could get, leaning ever so slightly towards the stoic wing of my dad, when the improbable - the impossible happened.

The wolf turned towards 'me' and leapt off the stage and ran up the aisle at full tilt. I did piss myself.

He broke the 4th wall between stage and audience, between the conceptual and the 'in your face'. It had been a barrier that I intuitively understood as sacrosanct, impenetrable. It was the thing we all use to this day, the suspension of disbelief, that allows us to feel the fear without it ever posing a real challenge.

As my comedic idol Rick Reynolds said;

"Ya know, we all know we're going to die, but how many of us really feel we're going to die?"

It was just a play but was a seminal moment in my life to realize that borders, real as well as esoteric, were all constructs and could be violated.

They could be broken and with enough fortitude, controlled.

Hesse once wrote in a collection of essays, called Wandering;

"There is nothing more contemptible than borders".

They're like cannons, like generals: if peace, loving kindness and peace go on, nobody pays any attention to them — but as soon as war and insanity appear, they become urgent and sacred. While the war went on, how they were pain and prison to us wanderers. Devil take them!

I decided to make the wolf my friend after that day, and to seek out and scale the walls and barriers of life ever since. It was a theatrical metaphor that translated in a very real way to me. It triggered a wanderlust that continues to this day and created an insatiable desire to see what's on the other side of the wall.

***

Day One

The very first day I ever set eyes upon the mythical Kingdom of Thailand, in late '82, admittedly a place that for all intents and purposes doesn't exist anymore, I set out to explore this fantastic and exotic new land on foot.

John Fengler

I was here no more than an hour and wanted to get from here to there as quickly as possible, because however exciting it was to be on this side of the road, unimaginably wonderful things had to be on the other side.

The problems began when I employed the New Yorker's credo of - the shortest distance between two points is a straight line.

This was a boulevard that had pedestrian overpasses set up with unacceptable distances between them, separated by an unbroken hedge-high fence that looked to be an easy vault. I crossed to the metal median, placed both hands on the horizontal pipe and began to hoist over.

Snapping off on both sides while I was mid-air was a twenty-foot section of corroded fence, that caused me to topple into oncoming traffic on the opposing side along with my fence section. On the way down the fence scraped a passing sports car, causing no more than a single brush stroke of paint in damage, but maximum terror in me.

The car lurched to a stop and two very agitated men emerged. Panicked and with no language between us, save for the universally understood inverted pocket, I expressed regret and handed off my current net worth, which was the exorbitant equivalent of about thirty dollars.

The guys couldn't have been more pleased, seemingly less so about the amount than the knowledge that I'd given my all to them. Standing alone and confused now I was approached by a Thai man who had witnessed this.

He spoke decent English and invited me to rest and clean up at his home which was nearby.

We walked the ten minutes it took to reach his family's hovel in Chinatown, and I was warmly greeted by the several generations of people who all shared this room. They began cutting up fruit and boiling tea, with young and old casting eyes over this exotic specimen from the west who was now in their midst.

Things were going well for a couple of hours then prolonged silences developed as conversation waned. I sensed that it was time to leave and thanked my hosts before beginning to make a departing gesture. It was then that a look of grave concern crossed the face of the man who had brought me. He said;

"Oh, but you cannot leave yet. We are waiting."

"Waiting for what?" I asked apprehensively.

"We are waiting for my brother. He works in Dubai, and he has money to give you."

"I'm sorry, I don't understand?"

"When you had your accident, I saw that you gave all of your money to those men, so we will give you some, so you will be OK."

I told him that I had given just what I had on me but that I had more (than you'll ever see in a lifetime, as it's day one!) in my backpack at the guesthouse. He blushed a bit and said;

"I know you are trying to be proud now, but please don't worry."

"No, really, I just arrived and have enough, but thank you so much for your kindness."

I don't think to this day that he believed me, but he let it go, lest I lose face. These people who had nothing but pride and jackfruit, had invited a stranger into their home for the sole purpose of giving what they barely had, and it was just a given for them to have done that. It was an act of kindness and generosity that set me on a life course and made me fall deeply in love with a now seemingly ancient people.

***

Cord-ially yours

Spent the day dealing with a world of air-con maintenance guys; filters, motors, Freon... all the stuff of living in the tropics. Made me remember the days of yore when coveting heat was the topic.

Back in the wood burning days of cold country, I bought a cord of allegedly seasoned oak from a seller.

Try as I might, I couldn't get the stuff to burn. I was miffed and wrote a strongly worded letter to the owner. Amongst the litany of scathing comments I made was the line;

"I wish my entire home were made of the wood you sold me. I could cancel my fire insurance."

Filled with self-satisfaction, I sat shivering but content with my vent. I also knew that I'd never be able to show my face at his business again, should the need ever arise, which of course it did about five years later. I had no choice as winter was upon me, and the competitors were unavailable. But who would remember an incident like that after five years anyway?

As I was placing my order at the counter, the owner came out and surveyed me. He saw my name and said;

"Did you send us a complaint letter about five years ago?"

I confidently replied;

"Um... maybe?"

He told me to follow him, which I hesitantly did.

As we entered his office he broke out in a big smile and waved his hand towards the wall behind his desk where my framed complaint letter proudly hung.

He continued the arched swing of his waving hand until it came to rest in mine with a hearty handshake.

He said;

"This was my dad's business before it was mine. We've not pleased everyone, though we've tried. But in all our years we've never received a better letter. I've been laughing at it for years and hoping to meet you one day. A cord of wood on me, and no hard feelings!"

***

Vintage point

I had a beautiful Parker pen that I'd inherited. Silver filigree - the works.

One day the connecting threads just wore out and the pen fell apart. I'd always heard that Parker pens were 'guaranteed for life'. I imagined it was an urban myth, but with nothing to lose I shoved it in an envelope and sent it off to the great beyond -some random corporate office in Wisconsin.

Six weeks later a box showed up at my home, with a note saying;

"Dear Sir, the pen you sent us has been out of production for over forty years. We have returned it to you for whatever sentimental value you can salvage and have included a replacement pen of a newer vintage. Thank you for your patronage."

A couple of days ago I got a wild hair and wrote a 'love note' to one of my favorite authors, who just released another international best seller this week. Mostly I write ditties just as an outlet, expecting nothing in return. Within twenty-four hours I received a very grateful and personal response. He thanked me for writing him and said;

"We love to hear from readers, as it's one of the only ways for us to know we have them."

I just love shit like this - a reminder that the world does indeed work and that under the seemingly oppressive weight of the Borg tapestry, there are still individual threads of life.

***

You, OK

Sitting in a bar in Siem Reap minding my own when a guy slammed down into the seat next to me;
  "This barmy local chick came back to me room, jumped into the sack and started saying;
  `You, OK?`
  I said I was fine and went to get her kit off, when she said it again;
  `You, OK!`
  I thought maybe she's givin' me a compliment, even though, ya know, we hadn't done much, but I thanked her and continued, as one does. Then she jumps up and almost screams in me face;
  `You! OK!!`
  I said; "sod this" and came down for a beer. What do ya make of that, mate?"
  "It's a condom brand here you know!"

"A what?"

"It's the name of the popular condom here. She might've been insisting that you have one or two before the festivities?"

"Yer' not havin' me on, are ya?"

"No, mate. And neither is she apparently. Cheers!"

***

A Christmas story

"Honey, why *falang* have Christmas? About first *falang* in the world, right?"

"No, there were heaps of us before that. Christmas is about the birth of Jesus. The first guy was Adam, but he didn't do such a good job, so they made another guy."

"Who his parents?"

"Well, God was his dad."

"God?"

"Yes, kinda like Buddha, only, ya know, bigger. He made everything."

"Like what?"

"Well, he made Buddha, and this wine glass, and syphilis."

"What syph..."

"Never mind."

"So who his mom?"

"Well, so God kinda had sex, but not really, with a woman who was a virgin after she gave birth. Oh, and she was already married to another guy."

"Oh, now you only joking me!"

"No really, and there's more."

"What more?"

"Oh well, then two thousand years of war, famine, intolerance, persecution, Donald Trump, and a few other things."

"Oh, why you say we believe crazy stories? *falang* even crazier."

"No argument there."

***

Jojo

When I was 8 or 9 my jet-setting dad shipped me off to sleepaway camp in Maine for the summer, ostensibly to hone my archery and canoeing skills. Really, he just wanted a break. Who could blame him?

One night, way back before the world was hermetically sealed for American kids, a young raccoon crawled onto my bunk and slept by my rolled up woolen blanket at the foot of the bed. It became a regular thing, and we were considered 'an item'.

I would steal packets of grape jelly from the mess hall to give him as snacks. We soon became best friends, and eventually snuggled face to face all night. The astonishing thing to this day is that it was allowed. I named him Jojo.

One day we were rubbing noses when, out of nowhere, he opened his mouth and clamped down with his razor-sharp teeth. His grip was unbreakable. Through a wail of tears I slapped at him to no avail, eventually having to pull his body away, his incisor dragging down through the soft flesh of my nostril.

I have a scar to this day. He somehow disappeared from our cabin after that, the counselor telling me that he went back to his family…but I still have the fondest memories of him.

***

Heroes

I got a summer job in my sixteenth year at the Antique Center of New York. I learned a lot about Wedgwood, Cloisonné, and pretense, which turned out to be way more valuable than the five bucks an hour I was being paid. My taciturn boss told me on my first day to;

"Never watch the gypsies. That's when they steal. Just turn your back and let them wander."

Sage advice.

About halfway through the summer he spoke to me a second time, and said;

"Hey, aren't you a Vonnegut freak?"

"Well, I wouldn't say a freak, but I really like his..."

"Whatever... he's standing right behind you."

Holy shit - OK, I was a Vonnegut freak. I turned to see a haggard, unshaven trench coat wearing man with sallow eyes. If he'd asked me for a quarter, I'd have given it to him. I immediately called my best friend and breathlessly stammered, asking what I should do. He said;

"Take something out of one of his books, man."

I steeled myself and took my teenage self up to him and said;

"Excuse me, but could you tell me how to get to Barnstable?"

His dour face immediately broke into a wide knowing smile. He stuck out his hand and said;

"Ha, ya got me. Kurt. And you are?"

The rest was a smitten blur. Sometimes it's OK to meet your heroes.

***

Beat It

Just watched a terrific documentary on the colossally creative life of Quincy Jones, and it inevitably brought me back to my formative days in NYC, trying to follow in the oil-slick, 24 fps footprints of my dad.

Dad was a well-known heavyweight in the commercial TV business of the seventies and eighties in New York, but his name closed more doors than it opened for me.
  "Wait, are you any relation to..."
And with downcast eyes I'd say; "Yeah, I'm his son."
  "Wow, you seem like a nice kid but, sorry to say, your dad's an asshole and I just can't hire you."
  "No problem. That validation just saved me a thousand bucks in therapy anyway."

I was strangely fearless in my job search and had learned film moxie early on. Many production companies were simply named after the directors who founded them, which provided an easy gambit for an 'in'.
  I'd confidently blast past the office staff and the queued-up starlets and head straight for the executive secretary's desk.

There was a particular powerhouse director that I wanted to work for, named Bob Giraldi. I was making fifty bucks a day in 1981 as a production assistant/location scout, which for a kid living in the West Village, just about paid my rent and filled my nose.
  I looked the secretary in the eyes and said;
  "I'd like to see Bob, please."
  It's a ridiculous and terribly insecure business, with no one sure of their job security from one day to the next, in the 'who you know' film world. This gal didn't know who I knew but was flustered enough by my confidence to say;

"Oh, of course. Please follow me."

I waited alone for a few minutes before Bob came in. He gave me a perplexed look and said;

"Who the hell are you?"

I stammered, giving a quick verbal resume while pleading for a job.

He laughed and said;

"Man, you got balls, kid. I like that, but I don't do the direct hiring... however."

And then he threw his arm around me and escorted me out to the main office and told them to plug me in somewhere. I worked on and off for him, as is the nature of commercial day shoots, for a couple of years.

We were out in New Jersey shooting an Arby's commercial one time, which as a bonus starred one of my childhood idols; Chuck McCann, who spent two days taking bites out of burgers, take after take, then spitting them into a bag that was held off camera by a guy with an even lowlier job than mine; the prop assistant. I went up to Bob during a break and said;

"Hey, I know I'm just low man on the totem pole here, but I'm curious... you're a terrific director, and I know you could have made this for a third of the production effort. Why so big?"

He smiled and said;

"That's why I like you, kid, you pay attention. You see those two guys over there? They're the product reps who are funding this gig, and they need to feel like they have creative input, so I way overproduce the shoot just so they'll have something to cut."

Sometime later Bob said he was leaving the NY commercial world to try this new thing called music videos.

Said he was going to do one called *Beat It* with Michael Jackson in L.A. and asked if I'd like to come along. It didn't sound like anything that would launch my career. As well, I had a bagel commercial lined up the next day with Morgan Fairchild and three days on a porn set in Times Square after that. My future until next month was secure, so I declined. I smiled and wished him good luck with the music video thing, confident that he'd be right back…

***

Backpacking daze

Hitchhiking is not a thing in Japan. I hadn't gotten the memo.

I had a vague idea of where I wanted to go but had an exceptionally difficult time catching a ride. Got loads of smiles and peace signs, realizing at a point that they genuinely didn't know what I was doing, until a fortyish businessman pulled over to give me a lift.

I pointed at my map with an earnest smile but quickly noted we would not be heading that way. And then I had my first traveler's epiphany. I figured that since I had no real destination, I couldn't be taken out of my way and that wherever I wound up was where I wanted to be.

We sat in awkward smiling silence, as neither of us knew a word in each other's language, until we pulled up at a suburban home somewhere. It was the days before cell phones, so there's no way he could have told the family that he was bringing a guest, but as we exited the car, his wife, mother and two children lined up outside the front door and bowed to welcome us.

I gave my host a confused smile when he pointed at my map, then at the dusky sky, then made the universal 'palms together head tilted on top of them' I've taken you to my home for the night, I'll get you to where you're going in the morning' gesture. His kids were bug-eyed at having a *gaijin* in their home. An extra bowl and chopsticks were laid out, and a feast was had.

Afterwards I was shown my sleeping area and ushered to the *ofuro*, or family bath. Stripped down and relaxing in the tub, the door suddenly slid open, and this man's wife shuffled over to me in her kimono, picked up a long-handled scrub brush and went to work on my back like it was completely normal. Apparently, it was.

The next morning my host drove me off as promised to a truck stop. He gestured for me to stay put as he went over to a truck driver. Returning with a satisfied smile he motioned me towards the truck and bowed his goodbyes to me. Our moment in time.

There's a Japanese Buddhist expression that I've tried for decades to adhere to as a kind of traveler's mantra. It's; *Ichi go Iche* e, which roughly translated means; You may only have this one encounter, so make it as full and complete as you can.

"The cultural concept of treasuring the unrepeatable nature of a moment."

***

John Fengler

Tuk Tuk

These little imported motorized Indian rickshaws, essentially hair dryers on wheels are what pass for transport here in Cambodia.

Most of the poorly educated and impoverished drivers still have online banking as their payment method though via their phones, which also work as their navigation systems. Last night I took a seventy-five-cent ride for the ten blocks to where I was having dinner.

There are these little laminated cards that hang from the ceiling with scannable bar codes to input your payment. On the one side you are given the option of paying in US dollars, and on the other you can pay in Cambodian Riel. The exchange rate is four thousand to one. My fare was 3200 Riel.

It was dark.... I chose the wrong side. I paid this guy $3,200 US dollars - more than he's likely to make in his lifetime. I noticed it right away and emitted a sound not dissimilar to a tire being punctured and deflating immediately. His phone made a payment 'ding' to which he gave no response until hearing my hiss. He then let out a chuckle and said;

"Don't worry, I give you back in a minute."

And so he did, reversing the transfer and restoring my heart to its natural rhythm.

I thanked him profusely and gave him twenty bucks. He was ecstatic.

My dining partner asked; "Why you give him so much."

I answered; "Good karma".

***

Confessions

Bless me Father, for I have sinned. I felt up a nun. Well not exactly, but...

St. Peter and Paul church in North Beach, San Francisco sits on the sidelines of Washington Square Park which on any given afternoon is replete with poets, lovers, drunks and frisbee players. The church itself is an icon of the Catholicism that defines the neighborhood's history. That and the Italian immigrants who brought it.

We were dispatched for the ubiquitous and ill-defined 'unknown', which in ambulance parlance translates to anything from;

"Get this drunk off our doorstep", to;

"Multiple gunshot victims, send backup now!"

It is the most Zen of all calls and defines the best approach to them as well. Tunnel vision is the death knell of a good paramedic. We were called into the rectory, or the closest approximation to what I imagined a rectory to be. There were nuns there. Real 'Sally Field' habit-wearing nuns. I was in my storm trooper boots with a police radio, handcuffs, and sixty pounds of rescue gear on my arm. It seemed like a tread lightly kind of place, which was hard to do in our business.

The nuns escorted over to a young woman of about twenty-three. She had almost translucent skin that was punctuated with red blotches. She was sitting nervous and still. Her breathing was rapid and shallow. Her eyes were darting around focused on everything and nothing.

She had thick red lips. Too thick. Too red. She was attractive, no, wait, she was a nun. She had eaten a salad for lunch. It had little tiny slices of strawberries in it. She was allergic to strawberries.

We are trained to respond to calls with an objectivity and a focus that we could not be distracted from. Much as a soldier can take apart and reassemble his field rifle in the dark while scanning a forest, so we were able to multi-task in the same manner. Cardiac arrest on the pitcher's mound, with fifty thousand people watching you work on the Jumbotron TV? No problem. Multiple car pile-up, mid-span of the Golden Gate bridge with a thousand cars swerving this way and that? Stay focused on the call, man! But there is a solemness inside a church that permeates even the agnostic.

I knew this was hallowed ground. I was at odds with my job description which dictated that amongst all the other interventions that had to occur pretty much at the same time, I now had to bare the patient's chest.

There were clinical signs that this young woman was heading towards true anaphylactic shock. I was well-trained at shielding doubt, fear and revulsion. It was our inner tennis game. But the conflict was evident. Evident at least to the Mother Superior who sensed my hesitation at exposing the virginal flesh of this young woman's chest. My hands reached towards the buttons of her shirt but were held back by my mind, much as President Muffly Merkin's hands were in battle with each other in the film Dr. Strangelove. Mother Superior seemed to grab my mind with her gaze and calmly gave me permission. She caught my eyes with a knowing comprehension and said;

"You do whatever you need to do."

It was an extraordinary sensation to buck such an innately sacrosanct contract, and yet it was my job to do so.

While the crowd of onlookers muted into a dark peripheral cloud around me, I navigated the bows and zips of a uniform I had never encountered before. Slipping it open, I was washed over with guilt, arousal and fear. This was a real call. Her pale and soft chest, as I feared, had splotchy red 'wheels' as they are called. They are the signs of rapidly approaching respiratory failure. I was hovering above my life, watching myself observe the rise and fall of her flesh, noting the changing respiratory rate and patterns. My stethoscope was gliding around, listening for the tell-tale sounds of rapidly narrowing airways.

I saw the increased use of accessory muscles and noted with concern her collapsing veins which would make getting I.V. access much more difficult. And all the while sensing the absolute velvety deer antler softness of her distressed skin.

One of the many untold truths about being a rescuer in the inner-city environment is that eighty percent of the people you were called to respond to might well have taken the city bus with the same outcome. Of the remaining folks who really required urgent treatment and transport, only about ten percent had their lives in your hands. But those ten percent were genuinely in your hands.

Anaphylaxis is the most unnerving of genuine life and death calls. To a point your patient is critically alert and locks eyes with you during your treatment. They are dying, and only you can save them. Really only you. They know it, you know it, and they know that you know it.

You have to express hope, calm and confidence, while controlling your surroundings, planning for egress and performing a host of medical interventions, knowing that this call could all go to shit in the blink of an eye.

It is a spectacular unspoken contract of trust and gratitude. Delegating tasks to frantic and idle onlookers is the best tool I've found for defusing tension, theirs as well as mine.

I had a call to one of the projects once. It was one of those government subsidy neighborhoods that sprung up overnight and didn't make it to the map books yet. The call was for a child struck by a car in a crosswalk. We took a couple of minutes longer to arrive on scene as we, and they, would have liked, due to our unfamiliarity with the area. There was a mob assembled. An angry mob who took this as yet another slight on 'people of color'.
"You all'd been here a while ago if we wuz white."
While assessing this crowd, trying to gain access to our patient and quelling the increasing anger, I shouted;
"Ya know 911 is not color-coded."
This gathering storm of bodies and anger was closing in on us, maybe two hundred people strong now. One squad car with two ineffective police officers were at the periphery just trying to set up a perimeter. We were on our own as far as safety. We finally reached the child, amid taunts, jeers and threats. I needed to quell the danger of this scene quickly. I looked around for the biggest, meanest motherfucker I could find, locked my eyes on to him, stuck a dagger of finger towards his chest, and said;
"YOU!"
It was like a giant pause button had been hit, and the crowd froze. It could very well have become my 'Little Big Horn', my last stand. I continued in faux confidence with;
"Keep these people back so we can do our job."
It was a hail Mary pass, and I knew it, but it worked. In one swift movement I had neutralized the greatest threat to our safety and had made him an ally at the same time. I had given him control over the crowd. I could see him inflate with a kind of pride.

"You heard the man! Now you all move back and let him do his job."

Back in the rectory there was no such delegation to be asked for. Only a group of true believers, fervently hoping that their sister would survive this event, and a Mother Superior who was cautious yet supportive, watching my focused hands and conflicted brain as I placed cardiac monitor leads around the young nun's breasts.

My patient then shot me a panicked look of betrayal. Still hovering above my life, while continuing the tasks at hand, I thought that my nonprofessional thoughts had somehow been transmitted to her, hence her look. But what I realized moments later, was that it was the look that is reserved for the failure of rescue as she slipped into unconsciousness from lack of oxygenation. It was the desperate last look of betrayal at my broken promise to save her.

While not the preferred mental status, unconsciousness can increase the effectiveness of intervention, as the patient is no longer fighting, and muscles relax. As if my conflict and doubt weren't great enough, I then reached for my intubation kit. I parted her ruby red lips and slipped the long smooth metal blade through her mouth, pressing firmly down on her pink languid tongue until catching the glistening white sheen of her choir singing vocal cords. I then passed the breathing tube through them and into the upper part of her lungs. I had secured her airway.

We started an I.V. to administer cardiac and respiratory drugs and gave her bronchodilators, which were nebulized, that is, given in mist form, which had the effect of forcing the medicine into her shocked system.

The rest was in modern science's hands.

She made a complete recovery, thereby reinforcing her faith.

Science had helped reaffirm faith, and faith had helped reaffirm science.

And I, while no less the apostate, had a newfound respect for the trust that people who know the limitations of belief can imbue onto others.

***

My date with Tennessee Williams

The film industry is a perennially insecure place to work if you are an up and going nowhere young lad. Work comes in spurts ranging from a day shoot on a commercial, to the insidious 'security' of a three-month film production. You are always on the prowl to pay next month's rent. You can't be anything less than the best at what you do, as there are a zillion folks waiting in the wings to take your spot. Nature abhors a vacuum. You also can't be too good as you'll be perceived as a threat to those who brought you on, as they are in the same job search feeding frenzy that you are.

As you ply the Manhattan streets looking for work, your eyes get trained to spot unmarked trucks sporting a bunch of grip stands by their back doors, or a few scrim screens laying on the sidewalk - the tell-tale signs of a production.

'Aha, a job opportunity is arriving.'

Such was the case one blustery afternoon in Central Park, New York City in the winter of '82.

Crossing from the Upper East side to the Upper West, I went by the infamous Tavern on the Green restaurant. All glass, lights and prohibitively expensive menus. The shoot was fully in progress, so I lingered in front looking for a way in.

An affable southerner approached me and started to chat me up in a friendly but suspicious way. Everyone is suspicious until proven otherwise to New Yorkers. He said he was a journalist who was in town for various theatre related events he was covering, this being one of them. It was a Neil Simon film adaptation. We chatted for a bit, and I started to take my leave when he asked if I'd like to join him for dinner as he didn't know too many folks in town. My flags went up as that just isn't something that happens to young guys too much in NYC, so I made up some excuse to decline his gracious offer. I turned to leave when he tried to sweeten the pot. He said;

"Tennessee Williams will be joining us."
"Really?"

Well that changes everything. "Um, sure. What and where?"

"Well he's in town to see an Off-Broadway rendition of one of his plays, so why don't you meet us at the theatre and then we'll head off to dinner, say 7:30? 38th and 8th."

I raced home to my roommates and said;
"Hey, I'm having dinner with Tennessee Williams. Who the hell is he, and what did he write? And are you sure he's still alive, or is this a big ruse do ya think?"

My roommate Liz started jumping up and down screaming;

"Are ya' an idiot? He's an icon John; *Glass Menagerie, Cat on a Hot Tin Roof, STREETCAR!*!!, anything??"

So I spent the next few hours in a crash course on American theatre and southern gentlemen. I knew everything I needed to know about this legend, or so I thought. I arrived at the theatre and was escorted to my seat by my new friend.

It was a small venue with seventy-five people at the most in the audience. It was a one act play with Hume Cronyn in the lead. Shortly after I sat down, I felt a buzz in the room and turned to see Mr. Williams, I'd presumed. He took the seat directly behind me. He was everything my mind imagined an eccentric southern playwright to look like; white linen suit, longish whitish hair and a Salvador Dali-esque moustache.

The play began. It was a drama which had everyone rapt in full attention. I was busy looking around for behavior cues. Soon I settled into the story but was distracted by an unexpectedly playful tug of my ponytail. I turned to see the playwright watching his play but with a twinkle in his eyes and a smirk on his face. I was new to this intimate setting and chalked it up to; 'ah this is what they do in the theatre world. Note to self'. I received several more tugs throughout and honestly was strangely flattered at the attention.

It was a predominantly somber performance on stage, which was only occasionally punctuated by the playwright's own laughter.

Afterwards there was much shaking of hands, bowing and introductions. I was brought over for a proper how'd ya do by the man who had invited me. A small crowd remained during our handshakes when the terrifyingly inevitable question came up. Tennessee turned towards me and said;
"Well, what did you think of the play?"
I raced around my mind searching for something less than vapid to say, and blurted out;
"I was surprised that you were the only one laughing at times."
He seemed quite satisfied with my response, shook his head and ruefully said;
 "Yeah, I just wish it weren't so dammed funny."
We all exited the theatre, and I followed our group to a place called Manhattan Plaza, also known as 'Broadway's bedroom'. It is a federally subsidized residential building in NYC which was largely, if not exclusively, the home for performing artists. Just past the entrance was a large open-seating restaurant. I seem to recall close to two hundred diners already in progress. It was a cavernous room filled with robust and cheerful theatre folks.
We were a group of about six or eight. A couple of our group entered, and then just as Tennessee was queued up to go through the door, he held back slightly and gently cupped my elbow to allow me to enter before/with him.
I have goosebumps to this day regarding the scene that next unfolded. As he passed through the entranceway, a reverential silence falls over the whole room. The entire crowd turned our way, and four hundred eyes were upon us.

Without any set direction that I could see, everyone simultaneously slid their chairs back, stood up and gave the most enthusiastic and appreciative round of applause I have ever heard.

It wasn't until that moment that it dawned on me the level of greatness, I was fortunate to be in the company of. I was humbled and a bit scared. It was also a testament to the playwright's humility as everyone was comfortable around him. He was the consummate southern gentleman. The crowd settled down and slowly diverted their attention back to their meals. I recall Tennessee, whose presence I was now firmly attuned to, performing a gesture which to this day I have unsuccessfully tried to emulate. Every time a woman would get up from the table, he would partially rise from his chair and give the slightest of bows, in a courtly motion, excusing her to attend to her 'nose-powdering'.

If you put a gun to my head I couldn't recall the menu, but the conversation was light, energetic and agreeable. There was a lot of laughter. After the meal Mr. Williams expressed his appreciation and enjoyment to everyone in turn and retired to his apartment upstairs. It was in the last moments of a most memorable evening when my new friend, the journalist who had invited me, dropped the other shoe. I said;

"Hey, I'd like to thank you for a genuinely remarkable time tonight and for introducing me to an incredible man. Thank you again and goodnight."

"Uh, hhmmm, I, um, Mr. Williams has asked me to invite you for an after dinner drink up in his apartment."

"Did he now?!"

It was in that split second that every red flag went up in unison and I had an image of my roommate's incredulity at my ignorance.

"Didn't think we had to mention it, John. He's famously gay!"

An otherwise perfect event was now spinning into a profoundly awkward and uncomfortable one.

"Um, please thank him, but I think I'll head home. It was a terrific evening though. Thank you again."

It was then that an urgency began to emanate from him, and a touch of rebuke took up residence in his tone.

"Do you know what a privilege this was for you tonight? You... owe me this."

He was beginning to physically box me in, positioning himself between me and the exit. I pictured Tennessee filling brandy snifters and popping breath mints in anticipation of what I supposed was to be a foregone conclusion. My extrication dance continued but unfortunately devolved quickly into a less than gentlemanly bolt out the door. I remember hearing some discourteous epithets keeping pace with me for about half a block until the normally frenetic pace of another night in NYC settled in.

Regaling my roommates with my adventure, they listened with rapt attention until the end when Liz looked at me aghast and said;

"You mean you didn't sleep with him? What's wrong with you?"

A little more than a year later, while reading the Bangkok Post in my hotel room, I froze at a headline:

'Legendary playwright Tennessee Williams dead.'

He had choked on a bottlecap while lying in bed.

A bit more than a year earlier I hadn't even been sure that he was alive, and now for me, as is the case for so many, he had become immortalized.

***

A Christmas Carol

I was walking around on a lonely winter's night one Christmas week in New York City. I saw revelers streaming into a mid-Manhattan club, so I decided to join them.

I was blocked by two muscle bound sentries who stated in unison;

"No unescorted men unless you're gay."

Seemed an easy fix. I smirked and said;

"I'm gay."

Hip to my subterfuge, guard one said; "No you're not."

"Am too!"

It wasn't to be.

Heading down the block I spotted a couple of young lasses walking alone. I approached them and offered to cover their drinks if they'd join me in a nearby club. They said;

"Sure."

Smugly returning to the front doors I was again resisted by the guards that I had now nicknamed the Cerberus twins.

The one turned to me and said;

"Nice try, pal. These girls ain't with you."

I replied;

"But clearly they are."

Guard two then rejoined with;

"Thought you were gay anyway!"

They had what New Yorkers call; 'A real hard on' for me. It means that for whatever reason they just didn't like the cut of my jib, and no way I was ever getting in. And I never did that night.

But filled with an indefatigable need for Christmas revelry I wound up stalking a nearby apartment building where a steady stream of well-dressed folks was being buzzed in. Up in the sky around the twentieth floor, laughter and the popping of corks could be heard.

With nothing to lose I went over to the panel and pressed 20-C as I'd seen others do. A disembodied voice came over the tinny speaker and asked what the nature of my business was? I said;
"Oh I'm here for the party."
"Who do you know?"
"... I'm a friend of Carol's."
... Bzzzzzz.
Note to self; there's always a Carol at a party.

Spent the next couple of hours drinking above my weight, regaling the mostly New *York Magazine*, *Paris Review* and Madison Avenue exec. crowd with tales of derring-do and keeping them in suspense while spinning my *Talented Mr. Ripley* stories as far as they would go. Then a man came up from behind me and proudly announced my good fortune, that Carol had finally arrived. That was followed by a wink and a conspirator's smile;
"Still it is curious that she's never mentioned you before, but we've all got our secrets now, don't we?"
The expansive flat was a warren of rooms and terraces that were all accessible to each other by differing routes. You could access the kitchen by way of the master bedroom or by slipping onto a terrace and then skirting through the living room, the library, or the maid's quarters. I spent the next while bobbing and weaving from room to room, always keeping a watchful eye as well as my distance from Carol, until somebody exclaimed;
"Oh there he is."

And so began my twenty-floor descent down the service stairs and back onto the lonely frigid streets of New York, three hours before the hustle and bustle of secretaries and garment workers would vanquish the night.

***

My oh my, an MI

About a dozen years ago I went to celebrate the late Thai King's birthday in Bangkok. I was outside the Grand Palace. It was just me and literally a million other folks. It had become a bit of a tradition for me to try and catch a glimpse of the revered monarch as he passed by.

I was walking along a nearby canal when I felt a strange yet familiar sensation. And then I clutched my chest. I ran through a career's worth of signs, symptoms and algorithms and said;

"Fuck! No, not me, not now, this is for other people."

Pre-hospital care is virtually non-existent here and I was as deep in the weeds as one could get. I knew that time was essential and that there was only one facility with standards of care that I wanted. It was far away, and exponentially so, having to extricate through a million folks. The most expeditious way would have been to get on the back of a motorbike taxi, but I didn't trust my ability to stay conscious that long, so I flagged a *tuk tuk*.

Mostly out of breath I told him the hospital I wanted to go to. He said;

"Three hundred baht."

Holding my chest even tighter I paused, looked at him and said;

"Two hundred."

I will die here on the spot rather than pay a tourist rate, I defiantly thought. He agreed.

Off we went at an albeit snail's pace, as every road along the several mile route was filled to the brim with loyal subjects chanting while holding yellow candles. It was terribly unnerving, yet exceptionally beautiful and almost a perfect exit were I to engineer one.

Into the emergency room I went, eye-rolling all around for yet another stupid drunken foreigner with 'chest pain'.

EKG rolled out when all the staff went into professional mode with;
"Oh, you have heart attack *jing jing* (really)."
The next bit was a blur but included an incredibly lovely paper hat wearing nurse who proffered a pen with which I was to sign a consent form. She said;
"Is because maybe you die. You understand?"
"Yes, I understand."
And then I started crying.
The attending physician seemed embarrassed and annoyed at my tears. The lovely nurse smiled and asked why I was crying. I said;
"Because you just told me I might fucking die, and I don't want to die!"
"Oh, is OK, everybody die. But you lucky to happen today. Is special day."
That it was….
And that's yer tale from the Buddhist Lake Wobegone of Southeast Asia.
Spoiler alert…I didn't.
We all got it comin' though.

***

Closing time

"So yeah, I'm drinkin' what we call Jack 'n' Coke'. Whaddya' want? Maybe some cherry brandy, huh? You like that?"
"Up to you."
"Or maybe a Margarita?"

"Margary?"
"No, ya know it's a Mexican drink."
"???"
"Mexico. You know, the country just south of Texas!"
"???"
"So what do your folks do?"
"Sorry, don't understand."
"Your mom and dad, what are their jobs?"
"Oh, farm."
"Oh they own a farm, huh? What, a dairy farm or, huh what do y'all do over here... um rice, right?"

"Yes, they rice farmer."
"Great. So, hard work huh? What kind of benefits they have?"
"Sorry, don't understand."
"Well you know, things like worker's compensation, maternity leave? Ya know, things like that."
"Ha. You want go your room now?"

***

The Food Chain

The first time I met Ollie was during a sleepover at my house. I was watching a movie with her mom while sitting in the guy position on the couch; my arm tentatively around my date who would eventually become my ex-wife, my legs outstretched on the coffee table.

She got over her initial shyness and flew over to my big toe. She watched, evaluated and decided things were good enough to start dancing. I thought it a good sign that she'd relaxed enough to let loose and do a jig. I commented that I'd never had a bird dance on my foot. My date blushed deeply and said;
"Um, she's not dancing... She's um, well she's having a very good time with herself."
"Really? They do that??"
I spent the next eight years hanging out with Ollie. She'd do a celebratory flight around the house each morning until landing on the far side of my bowl of Cheerios where she'd spend ten minutes decimating one single 'O'.

After breakfast she'd fly over to the sink, as was our ritual, for her morning bath. It was a split sink which had a one-inch metal breach between the tubs that served as a landing strip. I'd make a thin stream of cool water that I'd run between my cupped hands, and she'd jump into them to flutter and preen.

There was an entire food chain in the house as well, with five cats, two dogs, and whatever furry woodland creatures happened to be passing by at the time. She ruled the roost over the lot of them, utterly fearless and taking no guff, even when firmly trapped in the jaws of one of the cats. She'd peck defiantly until released and then chase her molester to a hasty retreat.

One day while she was out and about checking the perimeter, I took a friend's advice and put a mirror in her cage, the door was always left open. She tuckered out and went back home on her own and was just settling in when she turned to her right and saw the intruder. A mighty battle ensued between beak and glass with neither vanquished, neither the victor.

I lost Ollie in the custody battle but did get my dogs. As if... The proposal was to put them in the middle of the yard, and that we would go to opposing sides. On the count of three we'd call them and whoever they ran to would claim ownership. I agreed. The fix was in.

I'd put bacon in my pockets. Don't fuck with my dogs!!

Sometimes I miss my little food chain.

***

Going with the flow

I was in Thailand with one of my wives… thirty-five years ago. We were enjoying a nice meal when she shot me a look that only an intuitive married guy knows. I was new to the kingdom. I ran down to the first pharmacy I could find, with no language skills whatsoever. We were a rarity back then... white guys. I went into a frantic pantomime trying to mimic my best charade of menstruation.

Not in a million years would a Thai man address that issue. The female pharmacist was clearly fascinated on all levels, her eyes joyfully locked with mine, when she came up with the items I needed. I nodded my appreciation, and she nodded what I took to be profound, way before it's time, respect. My ambassadorial and connubial responsibilities concluded. A win/win situation.

***

Letting Bayons be bygones

About thirty years before there were signs, garbage bins, and walkways, I was taken to this 'secret' temple for one dollar. I've never known where it was, but the Angkor gods have brought me back and I couldn't be happier.

The first time I visited Angkor Wat was in the mid-nineties. I remembered that it was maliciously hot and that the elephants at the grand entrances kicked up a lot of red dust as they lumbered down the unpaved roads. The temple grounds had only been fully re-opened since the mid-eighties, as the last Khmer Rouge fighters relocated further west. The land mines though, were mostly still in place. The trillions of tourists had not yet discovered this amazing piece of history, and Lara Croft hadn't cracked her bullwhip there yet.

The infrastructure that has withstood eight hundred years of war, weather and neglect, had not yet succumbed to the unchecked development of boutique hotels, that in less than fifteen years would begin to aggressively leach the water system dry. I pretty much had the run of the place then, with unfettered access to the myriad of passageways and chambers that comprised this massive former temple city.

One day I came upon two shirtless ten-year-old boys, who approached me with;
"Hey, Mister, show you secret temple for one dollar."
Always one to try and straddle the bravery/stupidity fence, I hesitantly said;
"Sure."
They led me down a narrow jungle path for about a half of a kilometer. At one point I had to take a leak and started to turn off the path. One of the boys caught my wrist and flashed his eyes and said;
"No, Mister, do not go, have bomb."

I then offered them an additional one dollar if they got me back out! My sense of caution having finally kicked in, ended abruptly, just as the jungle gave way to a rocky vine-covered clearing. The boys bolted ahead leaving me in the briefest of panics, but they then began laughing and running up and down the rocks which were about thirty feet tall. I walked to the edge of the clearing to get a better look at the rocks they had brought me to, in hopes of grasping the 'temple-ness' of these ruins. I turned around and found myself staring into three giant carved Bayon faces, partly obscured by vines.

This was truly a secret temple in the finest of adventure styles. One dollar well spent.

Twenty years later and truly no less magnificent, the now paved road that connects these carved temple rocks to the world outside ends just a couple of kilometers in the opposite direction at another 'rock of ages'; the Hard Rock Cafe. And once again I have occasion to respond to the question I always get while traveling;

"Have you ever been here before?", with my sardonic look and the answer;

"Apparently not".

Stopping into an ersatz souvenir shack/restaurant on a subsequent Angkor trip in 2000, I locked eyes with a stunning young woman named Choum. I was smitten. I lingered as awkwardly long as I could with her and her family until someone cut through my obvious tension and, in a refreshingly non-western way, asked if I wanted to take Choum to dinner.

I arranged to meet her in front of one of the only decent restaurants in Siem Reap at the time, the Red Piano. She showed up with a chaperone in the form of her equally stunning and minimally English-speaking friend. I put a gently guiding arm around each of them and entered the wide doorway of the restaurant. There was a portly American chap sitting near the front who saw my grand entrance. His American wife saw his jaw slack with envy and disbelief and... well I'm pretty sure his ribs have healed by now.

I ordered fish Amok for all, with soft drinks and a desert. When the bill came the girls started giggling. I asked what was so funny. One said;

"This first time we go to real restaurant and so funny how crazy expensive it is."

I said;

"It's four dollars for all of us."

She said;

"My mom make same for one thousand Riel." (About a quarter)

As we were leaving, and unsure how to proceed with this courtship, the friend, anticipating my concern said;

"Tomorrow, we go to meet family of Choum at the farm, but I think no problem for you."

"Oh good, that's a relief. Wait, what do you mean 'no problem'?"

"Oh, I think her dad like you and say you can marry her!"

"WHAT?? Marriage?? No, no this was, this is, only..."

"Oh, she meet you in public. Now you together."

Still don't know how much ruse versus tradition that was, but I made sure to sew some seeds of distrust with her dad just in case.

We did meet once again, exchanged photographs, pen pal addresses, and promised to wait for eternity for each other. Twenty years later I still wonder.

Getting there in those days generally involved crossing into the Kingdom via the truly no man's land of Poipet. The war had left the muddy and chaotic roads nearly unpassable, with deep ruts, craters, and boulders strewn about.

As I walked through the border gate, I was approached by a truck driver who offered to take to me Siem Reap. After we negotiated a rate, he pointed to a beat-up open air white pick-up truck that was about a hundred yards across an arid post-apocalyptic expanse that was populated by the cast of the Road Warrior. He turned towards me, pointed at his truck and tentatively smiled saying;

"OK, hold your bag close to you and run!"

"What? Run?"

"Yes. Don't stop until the truck. You should be fine."

Wow.

Arriving at the truck I found myself with another three or four wayward and equally shell-shocked backpackers all clutching their earthly goods. We piled into the truck and moved inexorably slowly, dipping in to craters and swerving from stones. About fifteen minutes later and another hundred yards further we were told to get out and wait for transport.

This had been the transport to the transport.

Eventually a local bus that had been commandeered by a couple of enterprising locals gathered us up and drove us to the red mud chaos of pre-gentrified Siem Reap; land of myth and ruins.

A land whose backward flowing river will hopefully continue to enrich a new forward-thinking civilization.

Lorne

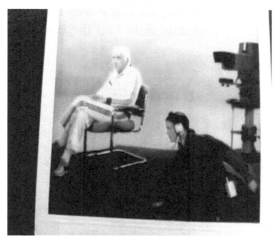

On the set with Lorne Greene years ago, he said to me;
"There are five stages in an actor's life, John.
The first is; "Who is Lorne Greene?"
The second is; "Get me Lorne Greene!"
The third is; "Get me someone 'like' Lorne Greene."
The fourth; "Get me a young Lorne Greene."
And finally; "Who is Lorne Greene?"

***

Kristen

I had to have some sort of interview in a back room of the embassy years ago. Everything was going well until the officer asked me what my ex-wife's birthday was. I said; "Man, if I could remember that we'd probably still be married." He laughed out loud and said; "Ok, we're done".

I've never been very good with that sort of thing except for my first love, Kristen, four and a half decades ago. I was on a date in San Francisco. We went to see a play. She was also on a date trying to get a second ticket for the very same play. We locked eyes and sparks flew, but there was no way in. And then a miracle happened. Her date only had the one ticket, and they were sold out.

I heard him mutter; "Shit, now what're we gonna do?" Without looking away from her, I said to him; "Excuse me, why don't you give me your one ticket and I'll sell it for you and call you after.

That way you can go see the other play down the block." He eyed me suspiciously and said; "How do I know you'll call?" Kristen without looking away from me handed me a piece of paper with her phone number on it and said; "Oh, I think he will...."

And that was that…no one the wiser. I was twenty. She still had homework. She broke my heart a year later, and a year after that she wrote me a letter saying;
"Dear John, I'm so sorry I left you. I knew that you loved me, but I was too young to understand the emotion. I learned so much from you, and because of that I'm able to be the best wife for my new husband, so thank you."
A bittersweet note if ever there was one. Happy birthday to my first love, wherever you are.

***

Effinbee

About a dozen years ago I was staying in a fairly nice hotel in Kuala Lumpur, Malaysia while on assignment…Was visiting an old girlfriend. Anyway…
We had dinner in the hotel, and it ran a bit long. When we finally decided to wrap it up, there was nary a staff member to be found... anywhere. I even went back into the kitchen. No one!
Confident in my due diligence I decided;
'Fuck it' and went up to my room.
Sound asleep about 1 a.m., the phone jarred me out of deep slumber.
"Excuse me Mr. Fengler, but you not pay your bill. We come to your room now to collect."
I said;

"If you come to my room now, I'll stab you in the eye with a fork" and hung up.

Checking out the next morning I was confronted by an imposing man wearing a general's uniform which had a bunch of stuff on its epaulettes.

"Mr. Fengler?"

"Um, yes."

"Effinbee."

Oh fuck - Malaysian secret service. Fuck fuck fuck...

"No, really, I tried to pay, and..."

"Yes, I understand. I am head of Effinbee."

"Yes, but..."

"Here is my card, sir. We apologize for the inconvenience last night. Your dinner will be comped."

"What? You're not arresting me?"

"No sir, I am F&B supervisor for the hotel."

"????????"

"Food and Beverage, sir. Again we apologize."

***

The Queen of Jaffna

I was hotel bound in North Dakota years ago at a conference. Doesn't suit me. I went down to talk to 'Billy' the van driver. I slipped Billy ten bucks and said;

"I need you to take me to the other side of town."

He blinked a few times and said;

"But there is no other side of town."

I smiled and pressed his palm and said;

"Billy, there's always another side of town."

Colombo redux.

My Sri Lankan odyssey a few years ago, as most of my travels tend to be, was wrapped around a single idea, a single goal.

The seat of the Tamil north has been inaccessible by train for close to thirty years because of a civil war which it recently emerged from. The rail line opened not long ago, and I wanted to experience it before it morphed into whatever socio-political landscape lied ahead for it.

Colombo railway station is like every chaotic Indian sub-continent movie scene you've ever seen. A maelstrom of travelers massing in overlapping queues. Each window hosting an alert yet detached civil servant, doing by rote what he and his father before him had done.

And as in the film, the chaos recedes to a slow-motion blur as eye contact is made with the ticket agent, and the crowd, a miasma of hawkers, shills and travelers recedes into the quiet din of background noise. I spit out at the Jaffna window at the exact same moment as an elderly Tamil man.

The agent had an eye for each of us and gave the same information to us both.

"I am very sorry, but we only have second class seats available on the Queen of Jaffna train."

The Tamil man and I both let out dejected sighs and simultaneously emitted plaintive pleas. He says;

"Are you sure there are no more third-class tickets?"

And me with;

"Are you sure there are no more first-class tickets?"

It was a humbling and poignant moment for me that belied the true class differences, as if they weren't evident enough. His was a plea about sustainability, mine about privilege and comfort. His, an effort to return home after the end of a brief hotel work contract and mine another self-indulgent voyage of discovery.

And the inequities of life continue, the illusion of commonality maintained by the belief that nine hours seated in a second-class train car together would be the great equalizer. But of course it wouldn't be.

"I'm very sorry, sir, Jaffna is not like other places. It is very traditional. There really is nowhere to go in the night."

"Billy…there's always somewhere to go…"

"Well OK, I do know one place..."

Now drinking lemon gin in a nicotine-stained basement with three whirring ceiling fans, two bare bulbs, a soft porn Bollywood movie playing in the corner with a dozen Tamil guys and a Japanese newspaperman; "crime section".

Life is good.

***

Inuyama

I recently came across a scroll that I acquired once, upon a time, in Japan. As I unfurled it, the memories associated with it came flowing back.

When I lived in Japan a thousand years ago, I got wind of a strange and magical place called Inuyama.

One day, I set off to find the elusive 'dog mountain', famed for its fertility shrines, with the hope of attending its annual 'penis parade'. Taking a series of switchback trains from Tokyo that wended me through the central province, I asked a group of uniformed schoolboys if I was getting close to the town. I said;

"*Ogata Jinja doko deska?*"

One of the boys tepidly stepped forward, looked from side to side, and then to confirm the location I had asked about, put his extended finger down at the fly of his trousers. Not sure how that gesture would play to his friends on the train, I awkwardly smiled and said,

"Yes."

The boys were relieved and pleased to have successfully communicated with this *gaijin* and gave me perfect directions.

And so I was able to attend the day long procession of the giant phalluses, as well as the 'sister' parade that honors the sacred feminine, which features unmarried women with hopes of becoming fertile and a vaginal symbol made of pink rice.

***

The Crossing Guard

My three biggest fears in life while growing up were; falling into quicksand, getting those nineteen-fifties rabies shots in my stomach, and public speaking. In fact, I remember seeing a statistic that said most people had public speaking as their number one fear in life and that dying was second. People would rather die than talk in front of a large group. Seemed reasonable to me.

In fourth grade I somehow wound up as a crossing guard in front of my elementary school.

It was a cool gig as I got to wear a plastic vest that had a metal fastener, and I got to wave a large orange sign around.

At the end of every week, all the crossing guard kids would have to debrief with our team leader, whoever the hell he was, and share our concerns and frustrations with the job. This was mid-sixties in New York City, a time of burgeoning sensitivity training, heightened social awareness and strained racial tensions.

We'd have to go around the room in turn and each contribute something. I was absolutely mortified, and that terror increased as the speaking circle began to close in on me. I raced around my brain for an issue to share and came up with my problem of the girl with the little black dog who would never wait for my 'all clear' sign.

I started chanting my rehearsed line to myself over and over, in hopes of being pitch perfect when my time came;

"There's a girl with a little black dog... there's a girl with a little black dog..."

And then my moment of reckoning came. All eyes were upon me when the crossing guard chief turned towards me and said;

"And what do you have to share, Johnny?"

The blood pumped into my face, my stomach tightened, when in a rush I blurted out;

"There's a little black girl with a dog."

It was my most feared transgression, the absolute worst thing in my mind that I could have said. I believed it would have been seen as a spotlight onto my soul and that I'd be branded a racist forever.

I stammered uncontrollably, saying;

"No, no, no, I didn't mean..."

And then the recess bell rang and the whole group shot off in the blink of an eye to the playground. I sat there stunned and speechless, until my friend Willie came over. I braced for reproach from him, when he said with a stern face;

"Hey man, that girl with the dog ain't black! You want to go get some French fries?"

And in that instant, all was good again in the inner city.

***

Liberal Religious Youth Camp

I was handed a flyer in Central Park one fine spring day in '73 by a lovely fringe wearing lass. She gave me an effervescent smile and told me to come to 'LRY' camp in Virginia.

Being a New Yorker I was wary of flyers, as well as offers of any kind from anyone. But being sixteen and filled with wanderlust, and more truthfully just lust, I went home and told my folks I was going camping with friends, then took a bus to the interstate.

I had never hitch-hiked before and wasn't even sure how far Virginia was from NYC, but what could go wrong? Turns out nothing did. I got a series of rides ranging from a would-be pedophile in a Cadillac, to a toothless farmer who was shuttling corn that;

"Needs some help unloadin' if yer willing, but I'll getcha near to where ya wanna be in Virginia."

Receiving my final lift in a VW camper-van full of LRY festival goers I arrived. At the entrance gate that sported a tent-lined lake behind it, I was greeted by Heather who was wearing nothing but a smile.

She asked for my hand, which I dutifully stuck out.

She jangled through a few bottles of nail polish in a side purse, settled on gray and painted my thumbnail, then said I was in the gray group for kitchen duties. Heather then asked me to stick out my tongue onto which she gently placed a hit of windowpane and told me to have a good weekend.

And there ya go. I was nothing if not compliant to the demands of a smile-wearing Heather.

Trundling down to the lake to pitch my tent I saw that not one of the thousand or so festival attendees was wearing a thing they weren't born with. Settling into my makeshift campsite I noticed all the emerging New England fall colors which I thought odd to see in the spring in Virginia.

The colors kept on coming.

I became self-conscious of being the only one dressed, so I started boldly assimilating by whipping off my t-shirt and, by the time I left after the weekend, I'd successfully managed to undo the top three buttons of my jeans.

More than forty years later I still had no idea what the nature of the gathering was other than the obvious, what it represented or who sponsored it. Three hits of acid later and a girl named Suzy, I had only been asked to peel one potato and don't ever remember returning to my tent.

I don't think I ever actually returned to my tent after that weekend.

***

Paris memories

Stumbled into Samir's Falafel house for a booze absorbing Kefta late last night. My new young friend was Hercule;
"Ha, is because I am strong, see", greeted me with a broad smile and a ghetto hand grip, the combination of moves I didn't know.
He immediately pulled me aside, flashed the conspirator's smile and said;
"Listen John, ze other day when I meet you, and you fill my head wif Thailand, well not ten minute after you leave, you won't believe, but zis beautiful Thailandese girl, she come into my shop. She tell me she is single tourist and looking for fun and a place to stay. So I tell her, you know, only kidding, that if she want a really good time, she could come up to my room. It is just above the kebab store. Incredible but she say she will, but she need a sandwich.

Ooh la la, I give her two. She really stay for ze night, Zen say she want to connect wif me on Skype. She say she like me a lot and want to wait there for me, but it is very expensive for her there. She live in nice beach area very near to Bangkok. She say a lot of foreigner come zere for ze good time on weekend. Oh John, maybe I follow zis girl and fall in love. She tell me how much her rent, and maybe I can send her some money before I come zere. What you sink?"

I muffled into my Kefta;

"Well a couple of felafels is the going rate in Pattaya, but..."

"I'm sorry, I didn't hear your answer."

"I said, I think it would be hard to leave your Farsi speaking dad alone in this shop. He would miss you."

"Yes, of course you are right, my friend. I keep my memory of my great Thailandese one night stand and dream again."

***

We'll always have Paris...

Viva la resistance!
I meet so many people here who wink at me and say; "They're so rude, huh?!"

I've been to Paris many times over many years. They do have a reputation for being rude. That is the cliché and, as in all clichés, they are born of a certain truth. It's a French word after all. I would say that Paris is like any other big, busy and thoughtful western city, in that it doesn't suffer fools easily. I grew up in NY, and I know this all too well!

I believe that here, as in everywhere, you get what you give.

I can speak passable French and so, flawed and without pretense, I am accepted and embraced. As well there are universal shared 'western' truths regarding body language and expressions of embarrassment, excitement, appreciation and fear which form bonds of their own.

In the span of ten minutes I ran into a guy on the street who reminded me that he had bought me a drink earlier and that his girlfriend liked me, adding; "but stay away!"; and an old woman collapsed in despair on the stairwell, whose husband is in the hospital, and won't be returning home. In short - the Parisians are courteous, polite, engaging, filled with self-doubt and delightful!!

Now excuse me while I re-adjust my scarf and enter this pub.

I'd been hanging out, as much as I do anywhere, at this great and dodgy pub outside the Bastille. It was old school great and genuinely dodgy. Real gangsters and characters of all kinds. Guys 'on the lam', outcasts, criminals, artists and writers. Some guy was checking me out, decided I was OK and dropped a picnic basket onto my table. The bar was crowded - French underground, Algerians, Tunisians, and Iranians - buying and selling visas, avoiding ex-wives, debtors and old business partners., The guy looked this way and that, before pulling back the cloth cover on his basket.

I was thinking;

'Great, it's gonna be some kidnapped infant, or a block of opium, maybe a pile of stolen passports.'

Nope. Cheese!!

"You know ze markets, zey are all bullshit. Zis is ze correct word, no? Zey get zer cheese from the same farms. Is different areas yes, but zey distribute ze same. I 'ave no store, so I am much cheaper. Yes, is not strictly speaking legal, but...."

"Alright, listen here, pal, I'll take a block of Morbier, Throw in some Camembert as well, then scram!"

***

FEC's

Guiding a pair of new eyes through Hong Kong, remembering what my old eyes first saw.

For any of you who were 'fortunate' enough to experience Chungking Mansion back in the 80's ($2 a night), I'm astonished to report that it has still not burned down.

The only official currency for foreigners to use in Reagan era China were the crisp, printed in English, FEC's; or Foreign Exchange Certificates. These were gameboard-sized bills that made you feel like the proud owner of Baltic Place rather than an off the beaten path traveler.

They also had virtually no practical value and were not known anywhere outside the limited regions one was legally allowed to travel to; the thirteen cities. The marginal value they did hold was that they were coveted by black marketeers as the only currency accepted in the traveler's 'PX's', where goods that were not available to Chinese nationals, such as Marlboros, could be purchased and then, in turn, peddled to the locals' black market. But if you wanted to eat food, sleep in a room or get from one place to another you needed renminbi, more commonly referred to as the yuan; the people's money.

When I was there in the early 80's the official exchange rate was four yuan to one U.S. dollar. The black markets' going rate was ten to one.

The actual physical renminbi had been in circulation for a long long time, and I'd never seen a bill that would have withstood the slightest breeze. It would oftentimes literally fall apart in your hands. They also ironically resembled Monopoly money by virtue of their size. They had pictures of trucks, ships, and airplanes on them, as well as a few indecipherable Chinese characters. I'd never met a traveler who had any idea of their respective values, nor which of the three had the greater worth. It was common to ask the uncommon traveler you'd run across the cost of such and such and to be given the answer of;

"Oh, a half a dozen trucks and two airplanes",

Armed with a ridiculous amount of the bills that were wadded up and stuffed into my various jeans pockets I ambled about on my sojourn across China. The streets were all dirt, the food stalls were no more than an old woman and a bit of charcoal glowing under a recycled oil can.

The Chinese on the street were scrupulously honest which took the worry and embarrassment out of payment, as you would extend both hands that were filled to the brim with play money when it was time to pay.

On one such occasion I found some appealing noodles, steaming and covered in a slick of sesame oil. The elderly woman meticulously extracted the two ships and the truck from my hands and motioned that our transaction was complete.

Shoving the wad back into my pocket with one hand while trying to balance my slippery noodles with the other, I must have dropped what to them was a fortune; a couple of bucks.

Slurping my noodles as I walked down the road, I sensed then heard the hurried shuffle of feet. I spun around to see an old man in his seventies, a hardened proletariat seventies, all but jogging to catch up to me. We were alone on the street. Without expression he lifted his arms and opened his hands to reveal a small cache of trucks, planes, and ships that I quickly ascertained had dropped from my pocket.

I was shocked, grateful and awkwardly appreciative. I thanked him. I thanked him profusely as I was hell bent on never being the ugly American and was determined to express my deepest sincerity.

It was during my third exuberant "*shey shey*", that this old man gave me a reproachful look, spun on his heels and stormed off. It took me many years to have explained to me what I could have done to offend him so.

In the Chinese way of thinking honesty and courtesy are givens. They are baseline and expected. To offer profuse thanks for something that was a given was to suggest that there was anything other for him to do but the right thing. It was an indirect insult to his integrity. I had insulted an old man on the street who was just doing what any normal person would do to someone who had dropped a week's salary on the ground. He was returning it to its rightful owner. I was from New York. That was not the M.O. of New York thinking I'm sorry to say.

I was to have a similar experience not ten minutes later as I arrived with my empty noodle bowl at an ersatz ferry landing. It was a glorified puddle, a water buffalo paddy that allowed passage from one strip of land to another, but a small bamboo raft ensured a safe and dry passage for the sixty second trip it entailed.

The operation was run by a boy and a girl, brother and sister I took them to be, aged about five and six. This was no lemonade stand, but the family business in agrarian China where everyone pitched in according to their abilities. The rest of the family were tending to the fishing nets and stick gathering nearby. The young boy showed me a truck and a ship by way of communicating the fare. It couldn't have been more than a dime.

While cheerfully handing it over to him, the young girl caught sight of my payment and surged over to us grabbing her brother's arm to prevent him from taking the bills. She started shouting at him and waving her index finger in admonishment until he relented and accepted only the ship. It seems that he was trying to extort an extra penny or two from the rich white man but was held to the rigorous standards of honesty that the party collective maintained.

Entering the mainland was anything but straightforward back then and entailed going through Hong Kong to get a group visa.

Standing on line for the X-ray machine at Hong Kong's old Kai Tak International, I was tapped on the shoulder by a dark-skinned and ruddy faced backpacker who had scraggly black hair. He spoke American English. I was at that point about four people back from the immigration guards who were all stern business. This guy asked innocently enough if I would do him a favor. He said that he was concerned that his baggage would be overweight, and would I be so kind as to carry his rolled up bundled sleeping bag through customs?

"It's only about two pounds"; he said.

Two pounds to my ears and proximity meant;
'Um no blindfold thanks.'
I turned to his innocent face, not wanting to insult him more than I needed to on the off chance this was anything other than a set up, but could only come up with;
"What? Are ya an idiot? We're inches from Chinese customs and you, looking like you, are asking a stranger to carry a two-pound bundle past immigration guards? Are ya serious?"
He was truly taken aback which was my worst fear, but quickly came around after being underweight and without incident after all. His name was Jeff, and he was from New York as well. It had never occurred to him that his request was out of the ordinary. He was a telecommunications worker for a large international company who had been awarded a year's sabbatical after seven years on the job. Word quickly spread around his office that he planned to travel around the world. He said that one day a bunch of office mates gathered around his cubicle as he was boxing up when one guy volunteered;
"But why would you want to go around the world?"
He blinked in astonishment and said;
"To get away from people who would ask a question like that!"
We became fast friends, and both realized we had the same agenda of finding one of the underground travel agencies that would give us solo travelers a bogus group traveler visa, which was the only way to get to the mainland back then.
And then we met Beth.
Beth was an attractive gal in that shy apologetic English way, with large breasts and a toothy smile who was on her own vision quest around Southeast Asia. Her figure made her a target of leers and curiosity. She seemed at ease with having Western escorts and we would become a traveler's trio across much of China. We also helped to quickly constitute a group which expedited our visa issue.

Kai Tak airport commonly known as Hong Kong International, was a unique airport and required specialized training for all international pilots. It entailed a dangerous grade and angle of approach which was unusually steep as the runways were essentially cut through the skyscrapers and mountains in the middle of the city. One of the conditions imposed upon Hong Kong was that there were to be no blinking lights in the city proper that could potentially distract or confuse the pilots. The result was that the night view of Hong Kong would appear as a freeze frame of modern lights; a cross between an Edward Hopper painting and a scene out of Metropolis.

It was with this remarkable light that we sat on the bridge of our diesel junk and watched Hong Kong recede into the blackness that would be our view for the next twelve hours up the Li River to the port of Guangzhou. As if emerging from a time machine we awoke ten thousand years before to the shouts and murmurs of Chinese dockworkers who were barely visible through the heavy fog that hovered over the riverbanks. Ghost ships in the form of ancient sampans, their sails the color of the muddy shores they skirted, would pop in and out of frame as the fog would break from time to time. As the shore approached our field of vision revealed a sea of bustling Mao suit wearing people in either Army green, or navy-blue outfits.

This was to be our port of entry to the People's Republic of China.
As we disembarked, we were led in a strict line towards a nondescript building. We were ushered single file into a corridor where the now twelve of our 'group' were made to line up opposite his or her respective backpack. A cadre of Army immigration officers entered through a doorway with one woman holding the leash of an imposing German Shepherd. We were glared at each in turn by unwelcoming faces.

The officer with the most things on his hat stepped forward, extended his arm and pointed directly at Beth who was standing shyly next to me in her ankle length skirt and ruffled blouse. He snapped;
"You!!"
We all nervously froze.
"You have...?"
My mind raced as to how his sentence would finish, ranging from weapons to drugs to tunnel blueprints. He continued his glare at her and said the most improbable thing I could have imagined.
"Bibles??"
Relieved, confused and strangely amused we all let out a collective sigh as Beth assured them, she was no missionary. The commander then motioned for the officer with the search dog to proceed down the corridor between traveler and backpack.
She had blessedly passed me and gotten about three-fourths of the way through when the dog stopped suddenly and lurched towards one of the men's packs. He thrust his head firmly into the pack as the group of officers closed rank on us and quickly drew their weapons. Just then the German Shepherd extracted his head and held a ham sandwich proudly in his jaws.

The captain was clearly flummoxed, embarrassed and angry. He gruffly waved his extended arm at our group and said;
"GO!"
And just like that our group cleared Chinese customs and, just as quickly, our 'group' dispersed to become once again the solo travelers we were...

***

Crying Uncle

My Uncle 'Dennis' lived in a two-hundred-year-old farmhouse in rural New Hampshire, which for folks from New England is redundant.

He had a herd of bison across the way, an alarm of geese that patrolled the drive, dogs, cats, and a large African Gray parrot which spoke English with a Croatian accent. The parrot's voice was a spot-on mimic of my uncle's long passed wife who had trained him.

At Dennis' end of days I went to keep him in good spirits, literally and figuratively. It was quite a drive to the state liquor store, and he was in no shape to make it. He'd lived an extraordinary life and would regale me from morning till night with tales of adventure from a time gone by. He would re-tell his life to me lost in a reverie and a wistful smirk. And occasionally, his wife would call to him through the parrot's voice, and he would be shattered every time. And then after a moment his tale would resume, and I would once again be transported to East Berlin in '39, New York in '43, Ethiopia in '62, and Miami in '75.

With an average lifespan of about fifty years, I can't help imagining that my Uncle's African Grey is still calling out his name somewhere with a Croatian accent.

***

Squeeze Inn

I infrequently frequented a favorite breakfast spot near Lake Tahoe in California for nearly twenty-five years. As far as I know, they're still cookin'.

They offered close to four hundred kinds of omelets, with a small spot on the back of their expansive menu conceding;

"And if you must have something other than an omelet...."

Aside from the charm, the food, and the locale, the biggest 'grab' for me was the gregarious guy who enthusiastically stopped at each table to greet customers old and new and to check their satisfaction levels. He never flagged in his duties as the consummate host. Then one day he wasn't there, and it was a palpable absence. I asked my waitress where the owner was, as it just wasn't the same without that experience.

She gave me a perplexed look and said;

"She's right there!"

I said;

"No, the real owner. Ya know, the lovely old guy who's always saying hello."

She cracked up with;

"Oh him? He didn't have anything to do with this place. He was just a crazy old 'volunteer'.

For more than two decades he had deceived me, lulling me into a false sense of family, security and bonhomie.

Oh how I miss that.

***

Dateline: Air Force One, 1990

"Respond to the Chief's office immediately, official business."

"Shit that can't be good", I said to my partner. "The guy who got ejected in that crash last week died, but that wasn't our fault, right?"

"Maybe it's because you forgot the gurney at the hospital yesterday?"

"YOU forgot the gurney, man!"

"Whatever, man. Middle of the day, middle of shift, yeah this can't be good."

Across town we drove, to the headquarters of the Health Department hoping for a pat on the back but expecting a boot up the ass.

We pulled up front and I turned to my partner;

"All right, ya ready?"

Independent thinking and autonomy are the hallmarks of an inner-city paramedic. They are the qualities that make us very good at our jobs. They also make us very bad employees, as rules and 'the chain of command' are the oil and water of street work. But in the end, they do exist, so into the Chief's office we went, guarded but humbled.

It was dark in there; curtains drawn and somber looks dark.

The Chief was standing at attention behind his desk. Flanking him on either side were the 'Men in Black'. They were caricatures of what anyone would imagine Secret Service agents to look like, wearing dark suits and darker sunglasses that betrayed penetrating stares through otherwise expressionless faces. Our curiously nervous boss cleared his throat, and said;

"These men are from the White House, gentlemen. You have been selected for a special assignment tomorrow for a Presidential visit."

Just then I caught movement from a corner of the room as an affable man in a much more casual suit made himself known. He calmly approached us, offered a confident handshake and a disarming smile in an otherwise clearly well-armed group.

He introduced himself as the MATCH for POTUS,

"But don't let the fancy acronym fool you. Stands for Medical Advance Team Chief for the Health of the President of the United States. He'll be coming in for a sort of meet and greet with the Governor tomorrow. We've seen your service records and thought you'd do well on our team for the visit. Now if it's all right with you and the Chief here, we'll borrow you for a few hours for a briefing. Nothing serious but we do have some procedures you need to know about."

As if knowing quite well the renegade nature of the paramedic personality he followed up with a knowing smirk and the advisory of;

"Would also be in your best interest if you followed their advice."

Our wordless sentries then ushered us to the side entrance and into a waiting black Suburban. We arrived at the service entrance of one of the big landmark hotels in the city. We went up to a suite and were then given this and that confidentiality and loyalty forms to sign.

"Just formalities you know!"

We were told that there were going to be quite a few dignitaries at this event, but that we were specifically designated to the President.

"For instance, if everyone on the dais were for some reason to go down… you would respond solely to the President. If someone next to him went down, you wouldn't move an inch!"

Sensing our confusion and discomfort he added;

"We have other people in place to handle the others. You are responsible for one person and one only!"

And then his seriousness melted into affability again.

He then brought us into an adjacent room, through the kind of door one always makes sure is locked when booking into a hotel.

Reclining on the bed and sofas watching TV were a half a dozen tracksuit wearing men, each with biceps that equaled the girth of the long canvas bags they were married to.

Our liaison gave a broad brush of his arm in way of group introduction, saying that these men were part of the protection detail and that we would be working with them and that they would finish up our briefing, give us the frequency codes for our radios, our passwords and procedures. He turned to leave and paused between rooms a la Colombo and said;

"Oh, and one more thing; Don't ever, EVER, get between these men and the President. Just construct an imaginary line in your mind and don't cross it."

He let that hang in the air for a moment, then followed up to our unasked question with;

"Because you're expendable."

And with that he was off.

We spent the next while being fitted and briefed, and reminded once again of the discretion that was expected. We were then bid a good day and told when and where to meet up with the motorcade which would be greeting Air Force One at the airport tomorrow. It was curious that we were returned to 'our normal programming', much as the announcer would tell the audience after every *Outer Limits* episode when we were kids.

That is we still had several hours to go on our normal shift that day and were expected to return to normal duty picking up elderly fall victims in the produce aisle of the local grocer, or ushering into the world the newest crack baby, who was born in an abandoned elevator shaft in one of the many housing projects in the city. And all the while we were giddy with anticipation over our secret assignment the following day.

We were the second to last vehicle in the motorcade with only a specially outfitted Highway Patrol vehicle behind us.

John Fengler

Air Force One landed and the President walked towards The Beast as it's referred to, the Presidential limousine. He then walked briefly down the line of his protectors for the day, shook our hands and thanked us for our service. It was a well-rehearsed routine but no less thrilling for it, despite my voting record.

We entered the freeway to town in a strictly spaced and timed line. As we passed a half-peeled Budweiser billboard that had two men up on scaffolds who were replacing it with a Cialis ad, one of the Suburbans in the motorcade peeled off and stopped just under the billboard.
Its occupants exited with pointed shotguns at the frozen men on the scaffold. Just as we were passing at the end of the motorcade the two men both nodded an;
'OK you may go about your business' to the petrified scaffold men and rejoined the motorcade replacing our follow car, which had then leapfrogged up to the next potential hazard.

A forlorn looking couple hovering over an opened map on the side of the road were greeted by shotguns that were pointed at them until we caught up again and, just as quickly, they were also released to their previous map confusion.
As we wended our way through the familiar city streets towards the hotel which had, arguably a limited number of practical approaches, 'we' were greeted with alternating groups of either supporters or protestors. It was curious to be on the other side of a protest sign in official capacity.
The protesters' insignificance was palpable. I immediately regretted that time I turned down Molly Striker's offer to join her in her dorm room in college, putting my libido aside for the greater good of holding a 'no nukes' placard in front of a previous administration's ride through town.
We exited our ambulance 'loaded for bear', as the Secret Service like to say.

That is, we were loaded down with all the toys of our profession and then some. Trauma kits, medical kits, resuscitation tools, oxygen bottles, cardiac monitors, a half dozen radios on different frequencies and even our standard OB/Gyn kit, which struck me as strangely superfluous for this assignment. But; "bring it all", means bring it all.

We had two 'minders' who were our block and tackles as we coursed through the lobby. It's an interesting thing that business as usual is still conducted on these hotel events, to wit, we arrived at the elevator banks and were joined by a couple of sweaty tourists and their luggage who were seemingly oblivious to the tactical takeover of the lobby. They started to move towards the opening elevator doors when our personal agents stepped in front of them and very politely but definitively said;
"Sorry folks, this one is for the medics."
I felt embarrassed yet proud.
Up we went to our suite to join our thick-necked compatriots for the day.
There was a banquet hall on our floor where this fundraiser with the President and the Governor would take place. Our entire floor was blocked off, as were the floors above and below. What had never occurred to me was that being there 'in case', meant we were to be banished to excruciating boredom out of sight from all the gala activities and to be remanded to eating vending machine food for six hours with a bunch of taciturn canvas bag toting Marines.

I got wind of the fact that the press room was also on our floor, albeit at the farthest end from where we were. The press has good food. Always one to try and finagle a better deal, I asked if there was any way I could scoot over to the press room for some snacks, with promises to bring some back for everybody.

It was a weak attempt to lessen my own nervousness that belied the seemingly relaxed ambiance of our little nest. My world was not likely to change today but, if it did, it would change profoundly. Best not to think too much about why I was there that day.

I was told that I could go anywhere on the floor. 'Great!'

I entered the solemn corridor and got to about the halfway point at the stairwell entrance. There was a metal detector set up that separated the Presidential side of the floor from the civilian/journalist side. The stairs and the detector were under the domain of another 'man in black', his dark sunglasses obscuring whatever possible expression his eyes may have had.

He made no attempt at greeting, nor did he even really acknowledge my presence. There are times when it's more awkward to not say something than to play the fool and interact. Additionally I was concerned that I would never be able to get through the metal detector loaded down with what I had on; badge, radios, handcuffs, trauma shears etc.

Seeing my apprehension the agent motioned me around the back of the machine, thereby circumventing my impediment. I got to the other side of it, turned to him and awkwardly laughed saying;

"Wow, this is kind of amazing that I can actually walk anywhere I want to on this floor and no one really knows who I am."

The Secret Service agent then looked at me with the most pitiful and condescending look I'd ever experienced. He half lowered his shades, furrowed his brow, bore into my eyes, and with complete disdain exclaimed;

"We KNOW who you are!"

It was with that withering epiphany that I realized the enormity of the vetting process that had preceded my presence and the depth and breadth of their security procedures.

"Oh my God, you know what I had for breakfast last Tuesday and the name of my ex-wife's childhood dog don't you?"

I received the closest thing to a smile I could have hoped for with that, before pressing on to the press room and then returning to my post without any further event.

Two weeks later I was once again called in to the Chief's office. This time the shades were open, and the air was breathable. I was presented with a letter on White House stationary from the office of the President's personal medical staff thanking me for my service and asking that I avail them of my services in the future should the need arise.

It never did.

THE WHITE HOUSE
WASHINGTON

March 2, 1990

Dear Mr. Fengler:

On behalf of Dr. Burton J. Lee, III and the White House Medical Unit, thank you for your assistance during President Bush's recent visit to San Francisco.

Although we had no need to utilize your ambulance, it was reassuring to know that it was readily available. Thank you for your participation in this "behind-the-scenes" endeavor.

Sincerely,

Jane E. Fraher, Major, USAF, NC
White House Nurse

Mr. John Fengler
Director, San Francisco Department
  of Public Health
Paramedic Division
135 Polk Street
San Francisco, California 94102

***

Got my Goat

A few years ago I was with some friends at an open air, dirt floor Vietnamese restaurant in central Laos. I joined late and my friends had already ordered. The waiter came by and asked what I wanted? I smirked and off-handedly said;
'Um, I'll have the goat, why not?', and then turned back to our conversation. A few minutes later the waiter returned to our table with a goat on a leash. He smiled and said;
"This one, OK?"
I turned towards him and laughed out loud at the absurdity as well as the apparent humor of the waiter and said;
"Ha, yeah he's fine."
And no sooner did my approval register, than the waiter, in the blink of an eye, slit the goat's throat with a blade he had held near in his other hand. It was the most present, the most thankful, the most conflicted meal of my life.

I ate with guilt and with gusto, with regret and with anger. I ate with the weight of a thousand goats that would be waiting for me in the Bardo. I drank deeply that night. Sometimes there is no quarter for recriminations, only appreciation and acceptance.

***

Forward pass

Found myself unexpectedly forty, unexpectedly single, well positioned, and in a particular frame of mind.

Suited up on a Saturday night in San Francisco's Marina district at a club owned by the now current Governor... Not a big fan of lines. This one was around the block.
"No way"

I told my pal;
"Just hang out a minute. Let's see what happens."
Sure enough the floor manager did his job and did his 'every quarter hour - check the line' thing.
I walked up to him and said I wanted to get into his club. He looked me up and down and gave a condescending smirk, saying;
"Who are you?"
I said;
"John."
Sometimes ya gotta go low.
He completely cracked up, and said; "OK John... how many?"
And we were in.

I was well dressed and fearless. Two cosmopolitans in, I was making out with a stunning twenty-year-old teacher with a fake I.D. Remember those days? It was desperado times. I boldly and uncharacteristically propositioned her, being twice her age, with half her confidence;
"I'll take you anywhere in the world you want to go... lots of strings attached!!"
She surveyed me for what seemed an eternity, then excused herself back to her friends.
'No harm, no foul' I thought, heading into my third 'cosmo', when she returned minutes later with;
"Jamaica!"
"Really??"
"You seem like a nice guy. These are my young and stupid years. Sure."
We conversed for a couple of weeks. In the end I chickened out, even though she'd re-doubled her commitment. Regrets, I've had a few...

***

John Fengler

Smurf Down

While I was waiting for my medic number back in the mid-eighties, I picked up an interim job at Marriott's Great America in their first aid clinic.

They outfitted me with a radio and a three-wheeled Cushman golf cart, which was the single-litter vehicle of choice for the narrow passageways of an amusement park.
Day one I got a call for;
"Smurf down".
Really??
Inside the various plushies that populate the park in summer, are 16-year-old girls who are sweating their brains out under thousand-degree costumes. This gal had overheated and passed out. The park had a policy that unless the patient was in extremis, we were not to remove the heads of the costumes lest the little ones freak out.
Zooming through Toon Town with my little red light, I arrived at Smurf Village and loaded up a life-sized teenaged Smurf girl onto my three-wheeled Cushman. How proud I was... Back at the air-conditioned first aid room, I got the bright idea to go out to one of the carnies and ask to borrow one of the 'knock the pins down, win a stuffed toy' mini-Smurf.

Back at the clinic I raced over to my patient's bedside and asked if she'd mind putting her head back on and posing for a minute. I grabbed the ob-gyn kit and placed the stuffed baby Smurf in delivery position at the young gal's loins and had a colleague take a photo. Hilarity abounded and I was the talk of Toon Town... for about ten minutes. I was summarily dismissed from the park shortly thereafter.
Management was not amused.

***

Sweet Meat
Dateline: San Quentin State Prison, 1986

The first thing you sense after you're informed about the 'no hostage' policy, as the tactile fears begin to replace the ethereal ones, is the bone shattering tremor from the gates that have just sealed behind you.

"We'll protect you best we can, but…"

I read a theory about autism once that suggested it represented a leap in human development. It postulated that over time the human gestation period will become shorter as the fetus has begun maturing at a faster pace. The mother is still stuck in a present tense evolutionary state, but occasionally, the baby is 'good to go', as they say, at around five or six months and starts imprinting, much as baby ducks are famous for, on its surroundings. The problem is that this now fully developed infant human brain is processing only amniotic sac and fluids, and by the time it's ready for its host/mother to deliver, it is unable to cope or relate to this new alien world.

That was how I felt in high school. I was just bored shitless there and predominantly sought refuge in the adjacent lands of the school where I could smoke pot and be on my own in peace.

The idea of moving on to college and taking a '101' intro course to anything was anathema to me and filled me with dread.

I was told that I could take graduate classes, but that I would have to be in a 'non-matriculation' status, which meant simply that I wouldn't get credit for having taken them.

That was fine with me. The first class I signed up for was called; Sociology of Urban Psychology. It sounded edgy.

The classroom was non-traditional in that it had no desks.

It was comprised of a single long oval table which was reminiscent of the SALT talks which had taken place just a few years earlier between the U.S. and the Soviet Union in the hopes of limiting the arms race. The oval was considered the most inclusive and non-threatening shape to decide the fate of the world. I was several years younger than any of my classmates, so I deferred to the farthest point from the instructor and any speakers that would come to address us.

On one sunny Northern California afternoon we were graced by two men who would give us an insider's view of prison. This was after all an urban psychology class. These insiders were not guards, not employees, but steel hardened felons. They were huge, with over-developed muscles and commanding stares. They were, as Arlo Guthrie humorously referenced years earlier; "father rapers".

They spoke at length about various aspects of the criminal justice system before they settled into the heart of their talk which was the life inside. They spoke about the adjustment period, the hazing period, the break-you period where - and just then one of the felons carefully scanned the room and locked his eyes on me. He lifted his tattooed oak tree of an arm, smirked and pointed right at me, through me as if throwing a javelin at my chest. He said;

"There! Huh, now that's what we'd call sweet meat!"

The rest of their lecture was inaudible due to the sound of my own blood rushing in my ears which drowned out any other sounds. That image, and the unrepentant confidence with which they expressed this new concept to me, instilled a level of fear that has never quite left me. And so it was with great trepidation years later that I received a dispatch to San Quentin in my first year as a medic.

It could have been an elderly transport from a nursing home to a hospital, or a fractured hip in the condiment aisle of the local grocery store, but it wasn't. It was;

"Inmate stabbing at San Quentin. Proceed with caution."
Really?!

The no hostage policy means that the guards will not negotiate with the inmates should they find themselves in a position of being overpowered and take someone - me, as a bargaining chip. It was an entrenched position designed to mitigate the threat. It was considered by authorities as a way to keep staff and visitors safe as they wouldn't be worth taking.

I was stripped of any obvious real or potential weapons at the entry gate, but still carried a treasure trove, a veritable arsenal which were the stock and trade of my profession. Narcotic antagonists, uppers, downers, needles, pins and a whole host of strangulation tools that were in my bag. State prison - where a toothbrush can be fashioned into a dagger and a dollar bill can be turned into a blow gun.

I was given the basic layout and the emergency procedures as I entered, while my equipment was being searched. The ambulance itself, which was of course left behind, was checked for explosives and stowaways with mirrors on long poles that swept the undercarriage. It was a laborious procedure which seemed to belie the urgency of the call, which had someone bleeding with an inability to control it. It was a process that would not be repeated on subsequent calls involving an injured guard or staff member.

And then the cat calls began.

The four armed guards who formed the human force field around me were powerless over the implied threats that permeated the air and penetrated my psyche. We arrived at the infirmary after following a blood trail through cell block D, to find a semi-conscious man manacled to a blood-soaked cot. He had long stringy hair, deep sunken eyes with the words 'love' and 'hate' tattooed on his eyelids.

There were a couple of buxom women flexing in black ink on his biceps, a skull with a syringe through its eye drawn on his left forearm.

Between the two in the place I called home, the place that is the domain of medics and junkies alike; the antecubital fossa, otherwise known as the place where the big IV goes, was the dark blue inked outline of a young lass's rectum.

This was the spot I had to hit with my needle. It was a disturbingly juxtaposed image, which in addition to everything else I had to disregard, forced me to have to essentially sodomize his arm tattoo. This could not have been more humorous to the staff, nor could it have been more unnerving for me.

His manacles were transferred to our gurney, and we retreated through a hail of taunts and jeers back to the relative safety of the entry gate. Just as I slid through the front gate an inmate boomed to me in a menacing tone, yelling;

"If he don't make it, it's on you sweet meat!"

I would have several other occasions to enter San Quentin again in my career and as with everything else in life, that becomes more and more familiar the more you do it, I eventually grew inured to the threats. And eventually there were sweeter meats in the form of recruits by my side to take the heat.

***

Proof of life

About ten years ago, I was on a Christmas holiday tour of Malaysian Borneo with my girlfriend at the time, who happened to be a petite blonde American.

We got wind of a good snorkeling island about 45 minutes off the coast and made ready to head to the official ferry dock.

On the way we stumbled upon a giant fish market which we found out had a second business of shuttling undocumented Indonesian migrants over and back for their daily jobs working in Malaysian resorts and hotels. These were primitive multi-colored local skiffs.

Always one to seek an alternative route, I befriended a dock worker who arranged a private boat out to the island. We traversed a half dozen skiffs that were snuggled up against each other and jumped from boat to boat until getting to ours. We were out about twenty minutes when the island came into view. At about the same time a giant cargo ship also came into view in Indonesian waters.

I didn't think much of it until we started aggressively tacking right towards it. I'm not a sailor and am ignorant to the tacking requirements of a small boat on big waters, but this was a deliberate direction and a very unwelcome destination.

We were already in an un-authorized area per State Department travel advisories due to insurgencies and recent kidnappings, and we were doing something relatively stupid.

I made a series of contorted facial gestures to my partner to alert her to the fact that our window was closing on redirecting the craft from what was becoming an increasingly alarming prospect. She gave me an 'oh you're being dramatic' look, which changed quickly to an 'Oh shit, what are we gonna do?' look, as the massive gray ship's side began to blot out our horizon. Aggression is not a natural action to a 'refined' Westerner; however self-protection is. My mind raced as I scanned our little boat and my hand closed on a paddle-less broken oar handle. And then the thoughts began spinning.

'Critical moment coming, have no choice, disable driver with plank of wood, send him overboard to certain death, commandeer an engine I am not familiar with and steer away from pirate ship to God knows where on a piece of land between Indonesian and Malaysian Borneos. Explain later.'

This was becoming urgent and very present, and oh so unappealing. Getting myself and my little blonde charge kidnapped was even less so though. I gave us another hundred meters and action would have to be taken. My girlfriend understood it all as I quietly lifted the plank to my side, fear and revulsion welling up inside. About sixty meters further our pilot abruptly switched tack, racing towards the bow of the ship, swung in front of it, and turned to smile at me while pointing to our snorkeling destination on the other side of the ship, oblivious to the past ten minutes of my concerns and planned actions.

It was Christmas day. Mount Kota Kinabalu loomed in the distance, as I paddled around a lacquer clear lagoon, gratefully getting stung by sea bees, safe in the knowledge that bad things do happen, but not today.

***

The human cannonball

All fourth-year medical students must attend several mandatory ride-alongs with the medics to complete their training. The same goes for many in certain parts of the Military. As is true for anyone unfamiliar with any profession, they don't know what they don't know. The docs tended to arrive with an attitude. They generally left with a different one.

We arrived on a shift a week earlier to find out that we had a 'doc-lette', as I lovingly referred to them, riding with us for the night. They can wow you with their book learned pathophysiologies of gram-negative intracellular diplococci, but they don't know shit about patient care or have any street sense, yet. This gal showed up in jeans and a t-shirt for her night shift. I greeted her and asked where her coat was? She shot back with;
"Nobody told me to bring a coat!"
I said;
"I'm guessing nobody told you to wear underwear either, but I bet you did. It's a night shift in San Francisco. Here take mine."

A week later this same shift we got a young Marine. I was a bit burned out in my career at this point and greeted him with the dismissive comment of;
"Just sit back and watch how the pros do it and try not to get in the way."
Childbirth in the field is generally the only call we get when it's not the worst day of someone's life. I've delivered a dozen kids, in less-than-optimal conditions, as befits the nature of the job. We deliver in alleyways, abandoned elevator shafts and crack house floors.

We even occasionally get legitimate pre-natal planning and care ones, when the taxi just caught the wrong light, or the Giants and the Dodgers went into extra innings and;

"Well no way we were gonna miss the end of this one..."

And those are the actual deliveries. Then there are the false pregnancies, the hysterical ones, the eighty-year old's psychotic break ones, and the;

"No way, dude. We only did it once, and it was like for two seconds, man" ones.

"Sorry to do this to you guys but you should be able to wrap this one up quick", our dispatcher always said when sending a crew on a late call.

"Fifth floor landing for the hysterical woman. You want Police?"

"No, thanks."

They always gave a pro-forma offer, we always declined. It's part of the bravado dance. Turning the corner on the landing we see an obese forty-year-old black woman, wearing bright pink spandex pants. She's lying motionless on her back, with a bare chested, prison muscled black man standing over her. He pays no heed to our arrival. Positioning is everything in these types of calls. You want to keep the route for your rapid egress open but don't want to block in any potential attackers either.

I knelt next to the woman and gently tapped her on the shoulder, making sure to stay clear of any sudden swing of arm, kick of foot, spit, knife, or projectile vomit. She snapped her eyes open, looked straight up at the ceiling, and proceeded to start rolling from side to side. She was screaming;

"Oh here it comes, I'm havin' a baby, oh lord I'm havin' a baby, oh it's a comin'." And then just like that she'd stop.

Mr. Clean as I'd dubbed our bald, gold earring wearing sentry, continued to stand menacingly still.

He was no immediate threat to us I deemed.

I turned to the woman, gave her my 1 a.m. war-weary sigh and said;

"OK, it's just us here ma'am, what's really going on?"

She gave me the universal 'dumb cracker' look and with insolent calm said;

"I tow'd you I was havin' a baby!"

I rolled my eyes and started to play along. It's generally the path of least resistance. I gathered what we call her 'pertinent medical history' and asked about her 'waters', her last menstrual period, prima/gravida questions - that is; pregnancies versus live births, etc. All the standard Q&A of a possible childbirth, tailoring my language to the patois of the situation. I had an intern once who was giving a physical exam to an elderly assault victim out in the projects. He was a good kid and had his book knowledge down, but he was new to the street. He got to the gentleman's loins and asked him if he was experiencing any 'scrotal tenderness', as the verbiage of his formal training had him do.

The old man scrunched up his face and said;

"What'choo talkin' 'bout, boy?"

My genial student again asked about scrotal tenderness. The old man looked exasperated and turned towards me. I smiled and said;

"Do yer balls hurt, man?"

He said;

"Shee'it izat what he wuz tryin' to say?"

Intern's lesson learned. I then said I had to check for crowning on our mother to be. My partner shuddered and shot me a look of;

'Better you than me, buddy'.

We had already done most of our assessment even before saying hello, as we are trained to do, gathering a phenomenal amount of information in a very brief period. We checked respiratory patterns and skin tone.

We checked pupils for size, reaction and movement, noted the absence or presence of incontinence, distention or flaccidity of jugular veins, checked for obvious trauma, paradoxical movements of muscles, telltale odors, drooling, guarding, etc., as well as establishing the level of mentation just through a brief exchange of questions and answers. And then with just a touch of a wrist, knowing that there was a presence and regularity of a distal pulse, that is, one at an extremity, which will tell you that there is enough perfusion to suggest a reasonable blood pressure. To the untrained eye we often evidenced a casualness, even an appearance of being cavalier, but it belies a full and ongoing assessment of surroundings and care for the well-being of patient, partner and family members.

Just then our patient had another bout of histrionics, replete with rolling, swearing, and screaming. And then again just as suddenly she stopped.
I said;
"OK listen, I need you to sit up and pull your drawers down a bit."
She shot me a withering look. I returned with;
"Listen I want to see this just about as much as you want to show me, but it's what happens when you claim imminent childbirth. Ya gotta check for a child."
I pushed it and reached in to grab her arm, to help her sit up. She said;
"Well awlright."
As she sat up, she revealed a pack of cigarettes with a couple of rocks of crack cocaine at its opening that she'd been laying on the whole time. Mr. Clean then sprang into action and lurched down to snatch the pack. On his ascent he shot a menacing glare at me. I jumped back, threw my hands up in the 'not why we're here, man' gesture, and said;
"Hey, we're cool."
He gave a departing; 'I'll deal wit you later bitch' look at our patient, then fled down the stairs.

My partner and I then smirked at each other, and both sighed loudly. He gave me a wry and mocking look, repeating my last words to the dispatcher of;
"No, thanks", referring to my refusal of police backup.
I turned back to our patient and said;
"OK, now where were we? Oh yeah, pulling down your drawers."
She then crossed her arms, jutted her chin outward and with great insolence said;
"You do it!"
Great. So I scooted her bright pink spandex pants down just as minimally as I could to get the information I needed. As I had suspected, no extra head of hair peeking out, no abnormal abdominal distension, nothing to indicate anything imminent. Then just as suddenly she went for her third bout of rolling and screaming, this time with her pants still down. And then again, she stopped.
We were losing patience at this point, and I said;
"Listen ma'am, it's 1:30 in the morning, and we've got five flights to walk back down. Happy to take you to the hospital (and finish this fucking shift), but you have to tell me why we're really here?"
She just stared at me. I said;
"OK, let's go, I'll help you up."
She then rolled up onto her forearms and knees, her butt in the air, refusing to pull her spandex pants back up. She raised herself halfway up to standing when BANG, a baby shot out of her like a human cannonball, ricocheting off the lowered crotch of her pants, snapping its umbilical cord and rolling onto the floor next to her. It was literally a bouncing baby boy.
Stunned and speechless my partner and I tried to grasp what had just happened. Our new mother continued her move to standing and without skipping a beat, said;
"I tow'd you I wuz having a mother-fuckin' baby."

My partner seized the infant and bolted down the stairs to hook it up to pediatric ventilation, as we now inexplicably had two patients.

I was left with Mom, who now was casually walking down the hallway trailing a traumatically severed umbilical cord from between her legs. I lunged after her and clamped the cord with my hand to prevent her from exsanguinating. She continued walking as I followed in a hunched Groucho Marx position, which was the only way to walk and keep leverage. I said;

"Where the hell are you going?"

She looked down at me smugly and said;

"I gots to get some things from my room."

"NO. NO you don't. You're coming with me, so you don't bleed to death."

I then turned her around and descended the five flights, gaining the downslope advantage of a step in front of her, all the while clamping her cord with my gloved hand.

My partner was now suctioning and ventilating the infant, which to our amazement was doing fine. I started an IV as Mom delivered the placenta. A passing patrol car stopped by to peek in at our road show. I glanced up with a smirk and asked the officer if he might rapidly drive us to the ER. He saw our bloodied hands, gave a small chuckle and said;

"Sure."

We delivered mother and child to the ER and were now back at the rig doing rock, paper, scissors for either clean up or paperwork. It was the eleventh and final call of our twelve-hour shift, when our stunned ride-along finally announced himself.

We had completely forgotten that our silent Marine had been witness to this disaster the whole time and, as he was told, stayed completely out of the way.

He had been witness to a colossal fiasco and had borne the brunt of my condescension as well. And yet all he had to say was;

"Man, you guys are awesome. I could never do what you do. Thanks for tonight and for putting up with me."

My lesson learned, humility restored, and a dozen years in still learning.

***

Chumley's

Chumley's was the real deal.

"The 1920's speakeasy became a favorite spot for influential writers, poets, playwrights, journalists, and activists."

Equidistant from the White Horse tavern of Dylan Thomas fame and my Morton St. apartment in the West Village, circa 1980, they were my favorite haunts.

Just listening to Girls Just Want to Have Fun on the jukebox, reminded me of a dinner at Chumley's, where an entourage of beefy bodyguards had a petite blonde as their charge. She was at the adjacent table to mine and lit up a cigar. I leaned over and politely asked if she'd put it out, as not only were we in a hundred-year-old historical wooden building, but I was trying to enjoy my steak.

Two-ton Tony leaned across the booth back and said;
"Ya know who this is, pal?"
I said;
"I do. Could you ask her to put out her fucking cigar."
He chuckled and decided not to kill me. I finished my meal and scurried away, but not before bidding Cyndi adieu.

Still, it is a good song.

***

Jimmy

About a thousand years ago when I first put on my travel water wings, my first big foray into the wild was to the U.K.

A wizened mentor told me I'd be fine, but to beware of anyone calling me 'Jimmy'. That meant that a head butt was coming. He said;

"If ya hear that, immediately lower your head, keepin' yer face outta da way."

I was in a pub tonight, quelle surprise, when an obtunded fellow (drunken asshole) began making his aggressive rounds. He was an East Londoner. There were many Thai women around so I wasn't at all concerned, as no one will kick your ass quicker or harder than a Thai woman. The owner got in his face and told him to leave. He mocked her and then spun around and got dangerously close to me, shouting;

"D'ya want me ta leave too? Well do ya? Do ya?" He was looking for it.

I ran through my Terminator screen of responses and actions and flashed on my first big travel tip. I looked him straight in the eyes, affecting my best Oirish accent, and said;

"Aye, settle down, Jimmy."

And wow, my gambit worked. He bowed 'is 'ead 'n` fucked off. And then the cops came, maced him, beat him and cuffed him. No, of course that didn't happen, It's Thailand. They laughed and put him in a tuk tuk and sent him on his way.

G'night Jimmy.

***

Black Sheep

"No, not Russian... Polish, but now maybe I have Somali accent."

"Go on..."

"I am humanitarian."

"Figured that much out already. I ruled out nun."

"Why? Nun also drink."

"Not in places like this."

"Haha, OK you correct. So I think you are writer, hhmm but not journalist? You look like you do more 'sophisticat' stuff."

"Hhmm, so... your face? Fresh wounds?"

"Yes, from VBID. Maybe you call IED, but zis from vehicle borne explosive. Zey give me ten-day holiday, so I come here, but you know it feel so, what to say, no edge. You understand?"

"So I guess the U.S. is off your list for a while then?"

"Haha, no I been in Afghanistan and Sudan too. I don't even try to go your country. Is Mogadishu for me now."

"You ever see yourself shopping in a Warsaw mall again?"

"Oh, such a good question. I went back for three days and can't relate. I already book my next 'vacation' in Kandahar. Maybe IED hit my brain too?"

"So, you're the black sheep of your family, huh?"

"Ha, I am only sheep, but what can I do?"

"You can have another drink... on me."

"Hhmm, jinkuya."

***

John Fengler

The other man from U.N.C.L.E.

I was lamenting the extraordinary spate of loss of friends and cultural icons this year to a pal, and his somber response was; "It's just our generation's turn to start dying, John."

And with it still feeling fresh on the poised and polished heels of Leonard Cohen's passing, news of Robert Vaughn's death roiled down the memory pike as well. But there was another Man from U.N.C.L.E. as well; 'Ilya Kuryakin' or David McCallum.

In the very early 80's I was doing some low-end production work on a variety of commercials and films. Many of the production facilities, such as editing offices tended to be in centralized buildings where a variety of works in progress would be housed/edited in the same location.

It was common to go to these editing room buildings and get directions to your project by asking for the working title of a shoot. Such was the case in 1981 when I was tasked with picking up the dailies; the previous day's shoot, for a low budget romantic comedy. I slipped into the elevator, squeezed past a couple of smartly dressed female execs and casually addressed the small crowd with;

"Excuse me, I'm looking for A Little Sex?"

The two execs began to recoil when a guy behind them smiled and said;

"Ha, it's OK, third floor."

I don't think that put the women any more at ease. Two reels of dailies safely tucked up under my arm, I got back onto the elevator and spotted a surprisingly short David McCallum on his way down. We were alone.

Living in NYC and especially working in the film industry, it was commonplace to cross paths with all manner of celebrity.

It was generally a non-event, and for the ones who crossed into mega-stardom there was an unspoken sense of respect and personal space that the locals understood and adhered to. The big exception being the old ladies who, as Elvis Costello recounts in his song; Watching the Detectives, would accost soap opera stars on the street as they couldn't separate actor from role and would lay into the thespians for their morally repugnant behavior regarding "Kate's unborn child. How could you?" or lambasting them for their callousness for "revealing Billy's adoption secret? Oh, Beth was so right to leave you!"

And there were the rare occasions when you just felt it was appropriate as you had a genuine... OK, you were just a fan and couldn't help it. So between the third and second floors I blurted out;
"Hey, you're David McCallum."
I was immediately mortified at my social faux pas when he looked up and beamed. He shook my hand and said;
"Why yes I am, um thank you."
The implication to me was;
'Nobody has recognized me in years. What a treat.'
My celebrity geo-file further ingratiated me when instead of commending him for his most noted role, my mind landed on an obscure episode of The Outer Limits from 1963 where he played a brilliant but mad scientist intent on speeding up the process of evolution. That seemed to strike a chord and he asked me to walk with him a bit where we continued to chat, with me tapping more arcane trivia from my brain.
"Oh and then there was some episode where you were drowning in quicksand and..."
"Oh my God, nobody remembers that one. I loved working on that. Did you know I designed the mix to make the fake quicksand? There was a lot of sawdust involved."

My detached mind was fascinated by just how accessible and vulnerable he was, and the brief exchange provided another in an ongoing series of life lessons about the beauty of connections.

The Japanese expression Ichi go Ichi e captures the ephemeral beauty of; 'one time, one meeting'. It is an indispensable tool to be embraced by any of life's travelers. An idiom that describes the concept of treasuring meetings with people. The term is often translated as "for this time only," "never again," or one chance in a lifetime, so make it full and complete.

***

Broadway Joe

National kid's day in Thailand had me waxing nostalgic.

In 1970 I lived in an apartment building on 76th and 1st in NYC. So did Joe Namath. Every evening before dinner a bunch of us kids would run plays in the middle of the street, with Chryslers as defensive tackles and streetlamps as right-hand guards.

Once in a while Broadway Joe would come home around then, walk over to us with his Hollywood smile, pick up our ball and say something like;

"OK, on 2".

We'd do our keystone cops run down the middle of the street, all eyes in the air, jockeying and jumping wildly in hopes of being the first to grab the spiraling football. Just as we'd receive it a half block away, Joe would wave to us and start to turn towards the smirking doorman of his apartment building. We'd all yell in unison;

"Hey, thanks, Joe".

Shit, am I old enough to have Mickey Rooney-esque urban jungle memories? Golly gee, I guess so, but it warms my heart to this day.

***

Regarde la sale d'attente

I am trapped in a room that's filled with people I hate. It started innocently as a mild dislike, but the scent of indifference that resulted from every flight delay, protecting them from my scorn, has worn off and left only the oily residue of loathing.

The haughty girl with the 'hey look at me' Bozo red hair, the Pattaya slob shoving fistfuls of Burger King fries into his face, closing it just long enough to give an open-mouthed chew, wiping the grease onto his polyester shorts.

The aloof English businessman scanning the room with greater disdain than I, while flicking a croissant crumb off the strangely placed mid-stomach monograms of his white Oxford shirt.

The shrill Chinese woman with the bad connection, screeching into her cell phone. The sugar saturated Scandinavian twins, flopping around in boredom with the boneless movements of spina bifida kids. The legions of stalled air hostesses mindlessly squeezing a never-ending supply of blackheads and the stunning Moroccan model who is steadfastly avoiding my gaze.

The wailing babies, the lonely planet group leaning upon their disassembled backpacks and forming a braiding circle.

The obsequious dowagers with their excessive bowing and wai'ing, the chador clad Muslim woman sneaking Cheetos through an opening, the implacably still monk sitting completely unfazed in his orange robe next to his red and white duty-free bag.

Most of all the wanker with the iPhone scribbling this all down wondering if this purgatory will ever end.

I quietly smirked at the bespectacled Harry Potter kid who was trying to teach his relevance deprived grandparents, who were feigning interest at best, about the new iOS features on his phone.

Silently mocking the forty-year-old Botox Bonnie from Santa Barbara who was having an expressionless sneezing fit.

Actively loathing the six drunken gap year yanks just back from the islands, fresh from their first viewing of The Beach, all wearing identical elephant pants with matching date rape grins.

And deriding the central casting caricatures of Gunther and Porn who were returning to Pattaya, he in his Hannibal Lector finest, she sporting the latest in faux Louis Vuitton.

Three hours I spent hating them all. All except these guys. These guys I liked.

***

Love and Haight

In 1977 during the gap years between academia and whatever lay ahead, I'd landed in the Bay Area of San Francisco. I wound up volunteering at the Haight Ashbury switchboard, the Haight Ashbury Free medical clinic, subsequently working a trillion rock concerts over the next twenty-five years for their Rock Medicine offshoot.
"OK man, we'll give you backstage at the Paul McCartney gig in exchange for you working two Billy Idols and a Scorpions show."
At the switchboard we provided community outreach, crisis counseling, referrals for legal assistance, food programs and, most importantly, housing. This often stretched to selflessly providing shelter in our own apartments to the legions of beautiful, displaced hippie girls that came through with flowers in their hair.

In the fall of '78 I took on a project of trying to set up a free lunch program at a local 'alternative' church of which there were plenty back then.
I was in phone contact with the founder who was very supportive and enthusiastic about working with us and made an appointment to meet with me in the following weeks.

And then he stopped returning my calls and I was given a bit of the run around from the staff at his church. I was quite put off, until seeing him in the news, in of all places 'Jonestown', Guyana.

His name was Reverend Jim Jones. His church was known as the People's Temple.

The rest is history.

***

Appalachia

1972 or so, I hiked the Appalachian Trail with some old high school pals for a couple of weeks between North Carolina and Tennessee.

One night we ambled into a real 'Deliverance' kinda town. I was a bit of a pool shark back then, and this place had a table.

We were wanna-be suburban New York City college kids, no hiding it, and that's the trick.

My pals were terrified as we walked in and implored me not to 'beat' anyone.

I said; "Hey, I play like I play."

Met a guy straight off who was table-side in a wheelchair. He had a tattoo that said; "13 and a 1/2."

I said; "What's that mean?"

He gave me a sardonic smirk and said; "Twelve jury, one judge, half a chance."

We shook hands, and then I cleared the table... several times.

My buddies were shivering in a corner.

It was either a shiv to the gut or a free round.

The bottom line - never try to be who you're not. Play your hand honestly and as guileless as you can. But always know where the exits are...

***

The Streisand effect

I was working at the 20th Century Fox film production office in NYC as a location scout. My buddy was a video playback engineer. He came over to me one day and said he needed to run an errand and could I "take over for a few". Before I had time to answer, he had split.

Moments later I heard the director's booming voice; "Where the hell is Playback?"

I sheepishly entered the room, a hundred percent unfamiliar with the equipment. The director got pissed off and stormed out, snapping; "I need this running in five minutes!"

I literally didn't even know how to turn it on.

Cursing my buddy under my breath, I got down on my hands and knees and started screwing around with the plugs under the table the machine was on. Over my shoulder I heard a nasally New Yorker's voice say;

"Why dontcha' try reversin' the polarity?"
I snapped back while slowly turning around and snarked; "Oh Yeah? Why don't you try reversin' your... oh. Hello Ms. Streisand."
Doh! I was never asked to do that job again.

***

Leave the gun, take the Cannoli!
January 1980, New York City

Out for Italian one night with a pal who said;
"I don't want to die this fat."
I asked him what his ideal death weight was?

For those of you who don't know - January is fucking bleak and cold in NYC. No room for errors in group planning. There were twenty-three of us gathered at one of my famous;
"Let's get everyone together and meet at…".
Infamous rather, being that, more often than not it was;
"Shit they're closed - again, John! Now where?? You promised you'd call first this time!"
This time they were open. It was Puglia in little Italy. Family style which meant endlessly long tables with whomever you were thrown in with - they were your family for the evening. Jeroboams of wine with no labels, monstrously tall piles of garlic bread, an accordion, a genuine fat lady singing and a waiter who performed pickpocket theatre with the patrons, seamlessly lifting watches, wallets and the occasional bra for laughs and concern.
And of course they'd smash many a plate on the floor for effect.

On this particular night there was a singular patron dining at a curiously detached table adjacent to ours.

An innocuous fellow until taking a fancy to Nancy, may she rest in peace. He leaned into our group and made a forward pass - out of place and out of time. So much so that he caught himself before any of us could register umbrage. I felt sorry for the awkwardness, terminal empath that I am. A lonely guy at a lonely table. I've been that guy.

I apologized to him in a curiously British way, in the way that they do for the transgressions of others. He left. We brushed it off and continued our plate smashing fest. When we finally asked for the big twenty-three diners tally, we were informed that the man at the table next to us had already picked up the bill.

Who was that masked man?

***

Dateline; Chau Doc, Vietnam, 2019

As an ersatz local entertainment guide at home, I'm often asked where to go. I give my pat answer that;

"It's not really where to go, but when."

I had occasion once, more than once, to be asked to seek alternate lodging for the night.

On this afternoon I drove off to Lake Tahoe, tail between my legs and stumbled into a set of 'corporate bungalows' that were rented out the eleven months a year the owners weren't in residence. I asked the rate for the night on a beautiful lakefront place and was quoted an astronomical price. I said;

"Listen, it's five in the evening on a Tuesday in December. There's no one in the world coming here right now except me."

The guy looked at me, laughed to himself and said;

"Yeah, you're right. How 'bout fifty bucks cash?"

And so, as it's been a truism ever since, here I am in a stunning top star French Colonial resort near the Vietnamese/Cambodian Mekong River border, reverse engineering a trip I made here almost twenty years ago to the day, when I wasn't in the habit of asking where the pool towels were and was once again quoted an inaccessible rate. I said;

"Can I ask you; is anyone else staying here tonight at the end of low season with a typhoon beckoning?"

"Actually, Sir, you will be only customer... Can offer you upgrade to riverfront view... and suite also... one million đồng, OK?"

"Forty-three bucks? Are ya kidding me? Where are the pool towels?"

***

Dateline; Chau Doc, Vietnam, 1998
Stamp of approval

The now defunct President airlines was a short-lived Cambodian carrier born in the mid-nineties, that flew for about a decade between Phnom Penh and Bangkok. The post-glasnost Russian crew were abrupt but efficient.

I was waiting in the main lounge area of Bangkok's Don Muang airport and struck up a conversation with an affable pint sized, t-shirt and flip flop wearing Khmer man, who was in town with his family to attend to some medical needs.

The plane was a 737 that had about a hundred and forty seats. On this flight there were nine passengers, five of whom were my diminutive new friend and his family. The ticket agents in their infinite wisdom seated all of us together in the three middle rows of the plane. I suppose it made the in-flight service for the fifty minutes that much easier.

My new friend was surprised to learn of my deep interest in his country, which seemed to ingratiate me to him. As we were landing, he asked if he could give me a lift to town? Wanting to be gracious I accepted, although secretly I was dreading the thought of being squeezed into the back of an overcrowded beater car.

As we were de-planing, I suddenly remembered that I would have to go through customs and immigration and fill out a time-consuming number of forms. I said that although I greatly appreciated his offer, I didn't want to hold them up, but that it was great to have met him. He gave me a cryptic smile and told me to give him my passport and to wait across the hall.

Pochentong airport now is a gem of modernity and efficiency. That was not the case two decades ago. Then it was a chaotic third world affair officiated by stern and wary uniform wearing military officers. I watched my friend approach the line of officials and saw them all nervously jump to attention and salute him.

"Who the fuck is this guy?" I thought.

He had a few words with a couple of the men, glanced over his shoulder at me, waved my passport around, and then walked back over. He gave me a warm Khmer smile and said;

"OK, let's go."

As we exited the airport a convoy of three tricked out Land Rovers pulled up. My friend motioned to the lead car and said;

"OK, this one is for you. I will be in the next one with my family."

"Who the fuck is this guy?"

I had a favorite squalid little guest house that I'd stayed in for years. It was on a dark pot-holed road on the edge of downtown. It offered big rooms, a hammock on the balcony, and was only six bucks a night.

And best of all it was owned by the most congenial Mr. Vuthy and his wife. I had never really considered just how down-market the place was until pulling up in a Land Rover. I also sensed how uncomfortable my drivers were to be taking me there.

The fleet pulled up in front with one man jumping out of each vehicle and taking a forty-five-degree stance. My host came over to me and asked if this was really where I wanted to stay? He gave me his card which seemed to confirm what I already knew about him, which was that he worked in the Agriculture and Forestry department. He invited me to join on an official Mekong tiger tracking project any night where our schedules matched. The family wished me well and the caravan drove off. I lost his card soon thereafter.

Mr. Vuthy then stepped out of the shadows to greet me. He regarded me in a way I had not seen before and said;
"Nice to see you again, Mr. John. Excuse me, but why you know big government official?"

I told him that he was just some nice guy who worked with tigers that I'd met in Bangkok. He looked at me as if I was a fool and said;
"No, he is minister here. You need to be careful with government people."

Fully aware of Cambodia's recent history and the understandable wariness people had, as well as their tenuous relationship with the government, I acceded to his concerns.

I spent the next couple of weeks touring the capital and environs before deciding to see if I could get into Vietnam by way of the river. It seemed a novel approach. Nowadays it is an over-touristed commercial route serviced by many tour companies. Not so back then. I got wind of a small cargo boat that was heading to Chau Doc, which was a predominantly Muslim inland port town in southern Vietnam.

I negotiated a transport rate with the captain of the little boat and arranged to meet him in the morning. It was there that I met Leila. She had apparently gotten the same idea as me, and we would comprise a passenger list of two people. She was an attractive gal, half Swedish, half Iraqi.

It was not common practice then, nor is it a great idea now, to inquire on people's business in the area past basic pleasantries. Most folks were up to some nefarious business in Southeast Asia, and it was mostly better to stay in the dark.

After sniffing each other out and sensing no threat we both relaxed and set off on our six-hour river cruise. We were surrounded by lush jungle several hours in when the captain said that we would have to go to immigration as we were now in Vietnam. He pulled the boat to the shore and threw a tow line around a bamboo pole. He said that we should leave our bags onboard and walk about a hundred yards down a jungle path to the immigration office, and then to rejoin the boat downstream after we were finished.

Leila and I alighted uncertain as to whether we'd ever see our backpacks again. The immigration office was no more than a shack which was staffed by a perplexed looking young Vietnamese officer who was very surprised to see us. I suspect he would have been surprised to see anyone as this was an obscure outpost.

He tentatively took my passport and flipped through it. He looked at me and then looked back at the document. He gestured excitedly at my passport and then pointed at me. I told him I didn't understand what he was trying to say.

He flipped through the pages again; this time more slowly and thoroughly and then shot me a definitive look.

"No stamp!" he cried.

"What?"

"No enter Cambodia stamp. How you can be here?"

And then the blinding epiphany of unintended consequences hit me. My affable Khmer minister pal who had expedited my entry into the kingdom, had done so without any thought as to how it might affect my departure. Probably wouldn't have been an issue had I left the way I came in, but here I was at a jungle outpost arriving by cargo boat, traveling with a half Iraqi woman and no entry stamp to the country I was now trying to exit.

I decided to go into indignant New Yorker mode, which is the fallback position for times when you have no argument, and your window is closing. It's times like these when military bureaucrats in an authoritarian regime work for you. They don't assign generals to these sorts of shacks, and the last thing in the world this guy wanted was an incident that would shine any spotlight on him. And I was well within my rights to be leaving without an entry stamp! Or so I had him believe. With great hesitation he hefted his stamp laden fist onto an ink pad and slapped my page. He then slunk back into his creaky wooden chair and looked away. Leila's paperwork was seemingly all in good order.

And sure enough our boat was tied up downstream waiting for us to continue to Chau Doc, our port of entry to the Vietnamese mainland.

**Chau Doc is noted for the Ba Chuc massacre - a twelve-day murder spree in April 1978 when the Khmer Rouge crossed the border and murdered over three thousand people. The attack was one of the reasons for the subsequent Vietnamese invasion of Cambodia.*

***

Immigration

So you arrive for the early morning opening of immigration and find that twenty people got there before you. But you see that no one had the moxie to grab the queue numbers from the box that's clearly visible on the officer's desk. You look around the room and deem the move 'safe', so you go to the officer's desk and pull out the ticket with the '01' on it, just as the lovely officer arrives and says; "Number One".

Your fellow expats blink in disbelief.

Questions - would it have been more ethical for me to have made an announcement, and then taken number 20 after their confused scramble? Or should I finish the paper over another cappuccino with the ninety minutes I saved by finagling?

***

The Powers That Be

I've never confessed this out loud before out of fear of being seen as, ya know... crazy.

I have a superpower.

I've used it successfully for years with the glaring exception of a Billy Joel concert in California a few years ago, where my incredibly great orchestra seat view was completely blocked by a seven-foot guy seated directly in front of me. Really seven feet!

And by seated - in front of me - I mean that he chose to stand for most of the show.

I glowered, glared and harrumphed for an hour to no effect. I visualized the 'eat me' cakes from Alice in Wonderland to no avail, and at one point came close to grabbing him and shouting;

"Could you be a little less tall right now? I paid good money for this seat."

Alas I found the error in my thinking and slunk back to the muted sounds of *Uptown Girl*.

Rick Reynolds once said that if he could have one superpower in the world it would be the ability to stare at the back of people's heads who talked during movies and just make them explode.

I met Rick once and confessed that although I lacked the pyrotechnics, I did possess a curiously innate ability to will people out of their seats. I would pick a spot on the back of their heads, usually a bald spot, and I would just force them to move to another seat. I even did this once halfway through a film. My powers so great that the guy left the theatre. I think it was during *Heaven's Gate*.

For people not yet seated I have an especially gifted power to glare at them, rendering them unable to choose a seat near me. I just tested this ability on my morning flight.

About one hundred passengers boarded the plane after me, and I scrutinized each one, allowing only a select few of them the remote possibility of becoming my seat mate, while forcibly rejecting the majority. One portly businessman hovered for a long minute in the aisle, looking from ticket to seat number and back again repeatedly. I stared so hard at the ticket in his hand, that I swear he saw smoke. In the end he seemed startled to note that he was in fact not sitting anywhere near me.

Oh 'lady with the teething infant' - keep walking - don't slow down - not your row- not your... yes!!

A couple of moderately attractive Chinese gals boarded, who I half-heartedly let my force of will down for, as it seemed inevitable that I'd be saddled with the company of someone given the sheer volume of passengers.

They passed by though and were followed by a long succession of clearly unacceptable folks. It's tiring work concentrating that hard on rejection but, in the end, so rewarding.

And in this case today it was especially so, having successfully orchestrated a vacant seat next to me.

***

October 17, 1989- 5:04pm
Play ball!

"I think you know a little bit more about this game than you let on, don't ya'?", the team manager once said to me.

I worked for close to a decade for a major league baseball team. I think it was my lifelong disinterest in sports that held me in good stead with management. I wasn't there to hob nob with the players. I was there to do my job. Well that and the perks...who doesn't like a guy in uniform on a hot day after a few beers?

"Baseball been berry berry good to me."

The team used to throw a big tailgate party in the player's parking lot after every home stand. All employees were welcome. One day I wound up shooting the shit with an affable guy, and at one point said;

"So what do you do here, man?"

He gave me a quizzical look and replied;

"What do you mean; 'What do I do here?'"

I asked if he was a groundskeeper or worked in the front office, or what? He scrunched up his face in disbelief looking for hints of irony in mine. He hesitantly replied;

"I play third base, man... you really don't know who I am?"

And as I confirmed my ignorance he beamed back at me, thrust out his giant hand and said;

"Kevin Mitchell, man. Pleased to meet you."

On another occasion I travelled with the team for a series of games in Los Angeles to see their archrivals, the Dodgers. Bellied up to the bar at the Hyatt one night I found myself in the second base position. That is, I was seated between the first and third basemen. I think we were all drinking screwdrivers.

A couple of ten-year-old boys emerged from the crowd wearing little pin stripe uniforms and holding baseballs and pens in the air. They got signatures from my two drinking buddies, and then one of the kids came over and tugged at my sleeve. He asked;

"Hey mister, are you somebody?"

I dropped my head in shame and said;

"Um, no kid, I'm not." Will Clark, the first baseman smirked and said;

"Oh come on, John, sign the kids ball."

And so, somewhere enshrined in some attic is a signed 1987 baseball with my name on it.

And two years after that I would find myself on the pitcher's mound on what was to have been the start of the third game of the World Series. It was billed as the 'Battle of the Bay', as both Bay Area teams, to the complete disinterest of the rest of the country, were to play each other in the championship.

It was a national event, so it necessitated several extra levels of security planning and procedures. I was in charge of medical for the stadium and was eventually outfitted with five radios, connecting in turn to internal security, San Francisco police, special operations, management, and a fifth one from the mayor's office;

"But don't ever use this one. This is for like, if the Martian's invade. Got it?"

"Got it."

The place filled to capacity with about half of the crowd being local, the other half from the rest of the world. On October 17, 1989, minutes before the start of Game, a 6.9 magnitude earthquake struck the Bay Area causing significant damage to both Oakland and San Francisco. Candlestick Park in San Francisco suffered damage to its upper deck, as pieces of concrete fell from the top of the stadium. The game was postponed out of concerns for the safety of everyone in the ballpark as well as the loss of power and didn't resume until ten days later.

The first thing I remember as the quake hit was a large boom as the power to the scoreboard blew out. There were about forty-five seconds of deathly silence as the place rattled and rolled, and then the half of the folks who were local continued with; "So anyway, where was I?"

The visitors who were not accustomed to the earth moving in such a fashion were understandably less chatty.

"What do you mean; 'Where was I?' We just had a big earthquake, man!"

"Yeah, and..?"

I ran out to the pitcher's mound as did most of the team, for vantage and safety. I looked down at my five radios and my eyes lingered on the special Martian one. I thought to myself;

'Well if not now, when?'

I summoned my nerves, gave my call sign and said; "There's been an earthquake at Candlestick Park. Prepare for the rapid egress of seventy thousand people."

The words had barely left my lips when I received the acidic bark of;

"Stay the hell off this channel unless it's an emergency."

I was taken aback until the crushing reality hit me. If this wasn't an emergency, what was? That was followed by the chilling realization that of course this didn't only affect the baseball park.

And then scattered damage reports started emerging of the bay bridge having collapsed, and of the Marina being on fire. But at the end of the day it turned out to be an orderly evacuation. People were either too numbed to panic or it was the colossally laid-back vibe that San Francisco is famous for. And all those disaster management classes actually paid off as I would join many of my colleagues for the next thirty-six hours running around an unlit city, tending to the needs of the citizens whose lives and emergencies continued unabated.

And a week and a half later the home plate umpire would yell;

"Play ball."

***

A boy and his dog

It was pillow talk, our fantasy wish list compiled while snuggling during post-coital bliss.

"OK, well I get Cindy Crawford of course."

"Yes, John, if Cindy loses her way and wanders off the runway one day and winds up propositioning you, you have my blessings."

"OK, so who do you want?"

"Well, obviously it would have to be Harlan Ellison."

"The *Boy and his Dog* writer, Ellison?"

"That's not the only thing he's written, John. You love *The Outer Limits* and *Star Trek*, right? He's great."

"Whatever - he's all yours."

In the very early eighties there was this new kid on the block called cable television, which was the access promise to the new world. All manner of non-traditional programming would become available to niche viewers.

A good friend of mine in NYC decided to produce a one-hour interview show, the likes of which are all too common now. He would pick a weekly theme, say from science, literature, or sports and get his hosts, Studs Terkel and Calvin Trillin to conduct the talks.

One week it was to be science fiction writers. My pal called me and asked if my writer and sci-fi fanatic girlfriend Nancy would help with the show, specifically on who to invite. She picked Isaac Asimov, Gene Wolfe and, of course, Harlan Ellison. She was thrilled, and just before showtime was asked to take a limo to pick Harlan up from JFK airport and bring him to the studio. We were both so excited for her opportunity. Not an hour later I received a phone call from an uncharacteristically awkward, Nancy.

"Honey, you remember that silly game we used to play, ya know, you get Cindy Crawford and.."

"Yeah sure, and you get... wait, what?"

"John, he's asked me to go back to L.A. with him for a week after the taping."

I was young, naive and stupidly idealistic. I thought; 'well, who am I to stand in the way of someone's dream?' And with my heart in my throat, I gave her my blessings.

A week later she returned with averted eyes and her tail between her legs. She hugged me and said;

"Well, to his credit he did warn me ahead of time. He said; "Listen, I am not what I write. I am not the guy you think I am from my books. I'm a mean, moody and abusive son of a bitch, especially to women"."

She then reached into her bag and gave me a consolation prize in the form of one of his anthologies. Inside the cover it read;

"To John, who seems to me to be quite a remarkable fellow."

Nancy and I continued for a couple of years after that and oddly enough would spend a fair number of nights in a midnight writer's circle in an L.A. diner, filled with odd characters and led by my new friend, Harlan Ellison. He rejected the monicker; 'science fiction writer', preferring instead the term 'speculative fiction writer.'

Had I the chance to revisit my decision with the wisdom and perspective I have today, I suspect I might not have been so generous.

As Captain Renault said to Rick in Casablanca;

"How extravagant you are, throwing away women like that. Someday they may be scarce."

Harlan passed away three years ago today, Nancy a few years before that. RIP to them both.

***

The Accidental Frottage

Squeezed in like breadsticks on the gate to plane shuttle bus, I felt a desperate need to scratch a spot on my back. With movement heavily restricted, I deftly slithered my arm down my side and began curling it up behind me towards the offending itch.

Just before reaching their destination, my curved fingers fully locked around the unmistakable B-cup softness of an attractive Chinese woman, whose breast was pressed up against me.

My hand lingered there for what must have seemed an eternity for us both, while I calibrated this new reality and the extrication moves needed to not cause any more damage. A sudden lurch of the bus only served to compound the tension, as well as the contact. The blinding epiphany of events became apparent but my corrective measure less so.

Do I acknowledge my inadvertent action and risk her humiliation or anger with an apology?
"Wow, sorry about that. That was a surprise for me."
To which she'd rightly respond with;
"Yeah, #Me too."
Do I shove the guy next to me and say;
"Hey, watch it buddy?"
Do I pretend it never happened? Or do I say;
"Hey, you're closer, can you reach that spot for me?"

Safely seated in my aisle chair on the plane, our eyes locked for the briefest of moments with a 'no harm, no foul' look as she continued to her seat, leaving me with one more traveler's anecdote to add to the handful I already had.

***

Cobbled memories

As do most folks here, I own like two pairs of shoes; Sneaker/loafers for 'dress' and a pair of sandals. They are sufficient but critical.

Yesterday one of my shoes suffered a catastrophic failure at a crucial construction point.

There's a guy I pass everyday who sits on an eighteen-inch-high block of wood. Next to him is a metal shoe form, a couple of ball peen hammers, a tub of glue, a few tins of polish, a spool of fishing line and a 1/8 horsepower polisher. As far as I know, he was born on that block of wood. I've never seen him not there.

I dropped by with my deconstructed piece of suede and rubber and gave him a forlorn look. He inspected it as if it were a Fabergé egg that someone had dropped. Like an art restorer examining a piece of fractured relief at Angkor Wat temple.

He peered up from his glasses, and solemnly said; "Tomorrow".

I just went to see him. He gave me my shoe, which was as good as new, and tentatively, hesitantly said; "Twenty baht?!"

That's about sixty cents.

I eventually got him down to fifteen…kidding - gave him a hundred, to which he lit up like a Christmas tree.

And just for the moment, in that moment, the Junta's happiness campaign was a great success.

***

Killing Fields

In 1983 I worked in a refugee camp on the Thai-Cambodian border named Khao I Dang. I got wind of a film production that was coming to town and specifically to the camp, to make what would eventually become the Academy Award winning film, The Killing Fields.

My source pointed me to the famed Oriental hotel in Bangkok where the producer David Puttnam was reportedly holed up.

As they were my formative days of finagling, I called over to the Oriental and in my most self-assured voice said;

"I'd like to be connected to Mr. Puttnam's room, please."

He answered on the first ring;

"This is David."

I blathered on about how I was familiar with the camp he was going to be shooting in and how I had a film background from New York and what a welcome addition to his team I would be.

"I'd like a job, please."

His response could not have been a kinder or gentler let down as he explained the part of the production concessions that limited the number of foreign nationals that could be employed and that unfortunately they were at capacity. He commended my moxie and wished me good luck.

Close to thirty-five years later I'm in Kampot, Cambodia attending a writer's festival where they've arranged for a screening of The Killing Fields in the old Le Royal theatre, which is a spartan cement walled room that's down a darkened tin covered alley. The film was to be introduced and followed with a Q&A by the producer, Lord David Puttnam.

I stood apart from the handful of attendees who were waiting to greet the legendary film maker. He walked into the alley wearing colonial mansion yellow slacks, a blousy white shirt with a red poppy in the lapel and a modest white beard. He chatted at ease with the few gathered fans before announcing that he'd like to look at a shop ahead of introducing the film.

He started to walk past when he stopped, turned and almost apologetically stuck out his hand. He smiled and said;
"Hello. I'm David."

I introduced myself and relayed my decades old story. We chatted a bit and exchanged warm knowing smiles about a time long past, and then he took his leave. And in those few minutes the power of the anecdote brought a half of a lifetime of memories full circle.

***

Feeling a bit 'homesick' today

Was chatting with an acquaintance in a pub awhile back, back when one could do such things… when he said;

"Ya know John, I've decided to leave Thailand and move back to New York for the remainder."

He was a man of some years, who'd been here for quite a while. I asked him;

"What could New York possibly offer, at this point in your life, that you couldn't in some way recreate here?"

He gave me the most thoughtful, and unassailable answer I'd ever heard. He said;

"Ya know, there are just some people I miss growing old with."

I was speechless and caught out. I smiled at him and wished him well. About three months later he walked into the very same pub and sat down near me. I said;

"Whatever happened to your returning to New York thing?"

He paused, turned and said;
"Eh, I got over it."

***

Tune in, turn on, drop out

I had the great fortune to chat with Timothy Leary once at an event at the SF Civic Auditorium, late 70's, if memory serves. Earth day? There were a lot of progressive and alternative thinkers there. That part I'm sure of. I'd wormed my way into an enthralled circle that was standing around him and waited my turn.

I told him about his influence on me during my formative years, and that now as an adult... He suddenly interrupted me mid-sentence, turned, looked straight into my eyes and said;
"Adult... is the past participle of the verb to grow."
Now that part I do remember.

***

Far Side

In 1983 I went to a book signing at the Booksmith in the Haight, when it was under the I-beam. There was an impossibly long line of folks waiting to meet our adopted local legendary cartoonist, Gary Larson.
I was about a thousand people back and remember stopping a woman on her way out and saying;
"Well, what did you get?"
She beamed ear to ear and proudly showed me the inside cover of her book;
"Hey Kimberly, happy to have you as a fan. Really pleased you enjoy my work. All the best, Gary Larson"
I stopped several other folks over the next half hour getting similar albeit shorter inscriptions.

When it was finally my turn, I excitedly placed my book in front of a clearly worn-out arm, made my greetings, and then walked back out onto Haight St. only to be stopped by another group of autograph seekers wanting to know what I 'got'. I opened my book and showed them;

"G.L."

C'est la vie. It was a thrill, nonetheless.

***

Boarding House

There used to be a great little club in San Francisco called The Boarding House on Bush Street, with a sister restaurant next door named Magnolia Thunderpussy's. They'd hosted everyone from Bob Marley to Billy Joel, to Patti Smith.

In the late seventies they were in declining health financially when a good friend of theirs offered to do a one-off set of fundraising solo shows in the club. This was an intimate place with I'm guessing no more than two hundred and fifty seats. There was no more highly coveted ticket in town than to see Neil Young and one that for the likes of an impoverished student with no connections was unattainable.

I'd been to the club many times as they were kind and generous to locals back then, offering dirt cheap student rates and sometimes free entry, as so many places used to do before the world changed.

I was going to school in a small Northern California town at the time of the show and saw a scalper's ad in the local paper offering in the order of two dozen tickets at inflated prices for the benefit.

That would normally have been filed under the 'none of my business' heading, but I felt a strange sort of kinship with the club and hated the thought of them having to lose 'life saving' revenue to someone else's greed.

I summed up my twenty-one-year-old courage and called The Boarding House. The owner answered. I relayed my tale and gave him the newspaper's info as well as the 'for tickets call this number' info. He tersely asked who I was and what my stake in this was?

I nervously stammered that I was just a random college kid who was a fan of the place and "jeez I hope I'm not in trouble for reporting this." He took my number and said he'd check up on my story.

About four hours later the owner called back to say that because of my lead he was able to recover all the stolen tickets, and would I please be his guest to see Neil Young and join for dinner at Ms. Thunderpussy's?

Wow!

I remember the entire set for the show consisted of a single totem pole, with Neil seated cross legged in jeans and a plaid shirt in front of it. And I recall a rapturous ninety minutes of sound where he played a few never heard before songs, including; *My My Hey Hey*. I was safe in the knowledge that I was participating in a legendary event.

About a year later the club finally closed. The building was subsequently torn down and replaced by condos.

***

John Fengler

Broads

Making lemonade out of the lemons of my temporarily self-imposed Florida retirement home exile a couple of years ago, I happened to dine with the most beguiling Helene one night, as my main charge was feeling under the weather.

I'm eighty-one now. The next ten years are the treacherous ones, I know. Most people here are boring.
   It's nice to meet an interesting person. I fled Nazi occupied Belgium, losing most of my family to Auschwitz.

I was a looker. I was very lucky. Things are different for you when you're hot. I was a bra and girdle model.

I met a man who was in the clothing business. We wound up opening a place in Hell's Kitchen and became known as the haberdashers to the stars.

We made a lotta money, let me tell you. Most of the big shots didn't come into the actual store but would order us into their hotel rooms.

The ones we really catered to were the Times Square pimps and the drug dealers believe it or not. They knew their threads and were very easy to deal with. The big shots wanted everything for free 'cause they were famous, like Sammy Davis. People think it was just in the movies, but the mob was a real thing. They came in for their cut, but they gave us protection... yeah... from them. Besides the Mafia payoffs, the celebrities, and the endless Studio 54 nights, there was booze, coke, quaaludes and a lot of pot. All the things these squares here wouldn't know about.

I modeled in the Copa and all the big clubs. I remember one time I was carried onto a nightclub stage while only wearing a bikini on a big platter by five men. Night club owners would regularly follow me into the dressing room to, ya know, cop a feel. All this 'me too' movement shit now, I mean I was just flattered they found me attractive. I mean that's when they were all 'pussy grabbers', not just this asshole we have now.

Fucked a lot of guys... a fair number of girls too - not bad but I preferred men. My husband... I was a trophy wife. He was twenty years older with a bad heart and ... well he wasn't in working order. Made me love him even more actually, but... he liked to watch, so that's where the girls came in."

"Like a refill, Helene?"

"Ah, yer gonna get me drunk and try to take advantage of me."

"I'm counting on it."

"Don't bother. You couldn't handle me. I'd kill ya."

"Hey, I die, I die."

"Ha, I'm double locking my door tonight then. You're a nice man."

***

Stuff

As a lifelong fan of saxophone legend Stan Getz, I'd been privileged to meet him on two very different occasions.

The first time was after one of his shows at the Saratoga winery in California in the late eighties. He stuck around for a meet and greet afterwards as the show had advertised he would.

He was understandably tired, and I suspect a little bored with this bit of the PR tour routine, but he slogged through it, signing whatever anyone put in front of him without even looking up.

I've never placed much existential value on autographs, but every once in a while, I just had to have one. I'd brought an album along that I loved and waited in line with the other sycophants to get it signed. When he saw the album, he put his marker down and held the cover out with both hands. He looked up from the table and met my eyes and said;

"Where the hell did you find this? I can't even get this one!"

I told him that I'd dug it out of a pile in a Tokyo music shop years ago. He gave me a wonderful smile and then grabbed his marker and signed it.

The other time I met him, years later, was equally as rewarding at a baseball game in San Francisco where he played the National Anthem, although not germane to this story.

I am dealing with the onerous task of disassembling my life and getting rid of a lifetime of things that have memories attached. They form the inherent attachment issues that plague any collector. A sofa that your dog used to sleep on, the jacket your dad wore to Hugh Hefner's party, the engraved champagne flutes that were a wedding gift from the sister of your first wife... or was it the second?

Things that by that very desecration become devalued to anyone else, serve no present purpose in your life other than to piss off your current mate, but seem criminal to toss into the trash. The few people I know who have, successfully, done this before me have all reported the same sense of freedom from their extreme makeovers, with the very act of getting rid of their things liberating their souls.

And yes, objectively, the album. Aside from having sounds that I would enjoy were I to own a phonograph, is just a piece of vinyl sheathed in a bit of cardboard, emblazoned with the squiggle of a magic marker. Would the memory of my meeting recede in the absence of the disc? Unlikely.

Bragging rights to fewer and fewer people who would 'get it'?

No. So what to do with it? Do I need the quarter I might get from a secondhand music shop in the local college town? Do I casually toss it in the dumpster along with the photos of long-gone relatives from Germany that I never met? Place it alongside the expired cans of uneaten soup? Next to the term paper about 'subliminal sex in advertising' that my professor gave an 'A+'?

And what of the creations acquired from friends, written by friends, photographed by friends, etched by friends? What makes the cut, and why?

And does not keeping one thing beget keeping it all? Does a single remaining attachment break the enlightened path you hope to wend and leave you adrift? Does physical detachment mean de-valuing its significance in your life? Or do I say;

"Come on, it's just one thin disc, I'll just wedge it between a couple of books on a friend's shelf. He'll never know it's there and I will?" Which in the end I did.

And what of the next memory, the next item of attachment? Where does it end, and when do the next attachments form anew in the endless illusion of ownership and memory?

***

New Porno

I bought some new porno tonight. More specifically it was 'NEW' porno. It wasn't my original intention but began as an evasive maneuver around a street hustle. There is no evasion really, as it's just one long gauntlet of scam. You always have to gauge hustle size on the business end of Sukhumvit and dance towards or away from it according to your comfort level.

Avoid the limbless beggars with their strategically placed toddlers and risk the paw and pickpocket of linebacker sized ladyboys. Skirt the ticket-happy tourist 'police' and get mugged by a gang of gingham clad Nepalese tailors. Ricochet around a drunken brawl between Aussies, and slam into a table of pleasure rings, vibrating anuses, harness-rabbit dong's, inflatable sheep called 'Love Ewes', and 'NEW' porn.

The 'NEW' caught my eye as I tried to overthink what that meant. Certainly there was nothing new about the mingling of bodies across the phyla and kingdoms of the sex video world. Were they just offering fresh faces on a tired old genre, special effects, a sperm cam, or maybe a new technology that allowed you to insert your own cyber porn image onto the screen? I had to know, so I asked for one.

The shadow play of sidelong glances over, I was guided down an unlit alley which was less than a car's width in size, to an endless row of rusted steel shipping containers that only became marginally visible as my eyes adjusted to the dark.

A lock was undone, a chain thrown, and a sequence latch lifted and swung to the side. The contents of the other containers had what; clothing, watches, muffled cries?

One side of the interlocking doors was flung open, and a two-watt bulb was plugged in, revealing tens of thousands of wrapped discs piled floor to ceiling. The sales guy pushed over half a pile leaving a waist high stack which he motioned for me to sit on. He told me to step in and take my time.

I said;

"You want me to step into an unlit shipping container in an alley in Bangkok that's filled with every illicit DVD on the planet while you stand between me and any possible way out of this thing?"

He said;

"What you looking for? You want kid, animal, gay, housewife, S&M? Have everything. Take your time. Buy ten get two free."

I let him know that I'd changed my mind and started to lean away from the steel doors. His posture intimated that his time had value, so I grabbed a movie and gave him the equivalent of a dollar. Turns out I had chosen wisely with *Assablanca*. A neo-noir twist on a timeless classic.

Not fifty meters from the flotsam and jetsam of regular nighttime traffic it had seemed a world away. Worlds within worlds unnoticed by the untrained eye.

***

Instamatic

Was having dinner with the kid last night, next to a table full of girls who were taking endless group selfies. We decided to photo-bomb them after a bit, which was good fun and made me think of how we used to do it 'in the old days'.

"So when I was a kid, about your age, you know before the internet and cell phones, when we just had film cameras, we'd sneak over, take someone's camera, take some rude photo of our butts, and then put it back, imagining their reaction a week later."

"???"

"You know, film cameras... like regular cameras, only they needed a roll of film... a canister... a little tube... with... film in it, that would let you take either 24 or 36 pictures, that you'd then have to take to a special shop, which you'd then have to go back to about a week later to get your pictures."

"... Really?"

***

Morning cup of Joe

"Wow, looks like you're really enjoying that breakfast there." I said.

"Oh yeah, ya know it's been a while. Been in the jungle for a year. Teaching hill-tribe kids mostly; Karen, Hmong, Yao, and Akha. Shit they can't hardly talk to one another 'cept for a little bit of Thai between 'em, and now… a little English. Got a hundred and thirty of 'em.

I'm independent by the way, not hooked up with any of those bloated fucking NGOs, or those self-serving religious groups. Just me and a bunch of dedicated and well-educated Thais on Royal projects. You know these are truly honest folks, given pretty good funding and they're trying to do some good. Happy to be a part of it, but Jesus Christ it's good to have a plate of bacon and eggs. I mean off the grid is OK I guess, but then there's really off the grid.

Sorry to ramble but haven't had a chance to have a conversation in my native tongue for a while either. Seen a few westerners; a SEAL team and some special forces types… on holiday… spooks I guess, but I don't cross paths with them.

I used to be in that game myself back when. Worked with helicopters in Iran during the revolution, then with the Montagnards in Vietnam. Used to be a common thread of patriotism that kept us all together, but these fucks, well I keep separate is all. Ya know the problem is they don't know why the hell they're here, or what they're really doing this for. Nobody trusts anyone, especially the yanks, so I just do my own thing.

Lotta folks over here ending their days on a *mea culpa* I s'poze, ya know, trying to atone for past deeds, not that we thought any of it was wrong ya understand, it's just that, well time teaches you a few things.

Heading back in next week. Re-supplied as it were. At least I got my identity back. Sure know how brainwashing works now, ya know, separated from everything you know that defines you. Learned a lot about myself and I know some folks would spend big bucks for an experience like that, and I'll tell ya what, it's worth every penny.

Well I'll be around for a little bit yet. Maybe I'll see you again. Name's Joe by the way."

***

Mount Audubon

In 1977 I hitchhiked across the US for the first time.

I was heading towards LA for surf, sun and beach bunnies. I lasted about an hour and a half after realizing that the progressive counterculture scene of San Francisco was where I was at. Somewhere in the Rockies I'd stopped into a laundromat to dump my backpack out and do some wash. There was a note tacked onto a board asking for a climbing companion up to Mount Audubon, in Colorado. I pulled out a quarter and called the guy. He had ropes, picks, and knew about altitude sickness. I knew nothing. He took me on.

The peak hovers at around 13,000 ft.

We made base camp for a night in Estes Park at 8,000 feet, and being a veteran of the Boy Scouts I was well equipped to make a hot dinner on my camp stove. Water was boiling when I threw in our mac and cheese and then sat back and waited…and waited…and waited, until my climbing partner came over and asked me what the hell I was doing. I told him that I was boiling water, but that for some bizarre reason, it wasn't getting hot. He said; "You didn't learn about physics in high school, did you? We're at 8,000 feet".

A cold dinner of dehydrated meat it was.

The climb was strenuous and exhilarating. He'd told me to drink five liters of water during our ascent. I told him that I wasn't thirsty. He said;

"No matter, your body is."

Whatever.

We hit the peak and I have never felt worse in my life, totally dehydrated with a pounding headache and generally hating life.

He grabbed my camera and told me to smile. I said I didn't feel like it. He said;

"I don't suspect you'll ever be doing something like this again. C'mon, smile for the folks back home."

After the climb I continued through the Rockies until wending my way towards the sunny beaches of California. I got to Crescent City, a coastal town in California near the Oregon border, having hooked up with a petty criminal to hitchhike with for a few days. We were broke and hungry and decided to stash our packs in some bushes and plead for some work at a nearby marina.

The harbor master told us to wait in his office for a few while he went to see what needed to be worked on. About ten minutes later a police car showed up and two officers came over, told us to grab our packs and then they put us in the squad car.

Shit, getting arrested for vagrancy I thought.

We sat in silence until pulling up in front of a diner. The officers got out and went to each of our car doors. As I was getting out, 'my' officer reached out his hand and slipped me $5. He motioned towards the diner, smiled and said;

"I know what it is to be poor. Good luck."

Brings a tear to my eye to this day. A couple of decades later I made a single purpose trip back to Crescent City to try and track down that officer, give him his five bucks back and let him know that he made a good investment.

I never found him.

***

Jackson Pollock

I was on one of my monthly forays to 'the Penh' a couple of years ago, dressed to the nines in a clean t-shirt and shorts. It was Saturday night after all, and my pals were performing at a little club.

All set to go out when I suddenly became woozy, and then noticed that I'd sprung a leak. Would be indiscreet to elaborate, but my white shorts now looked like a Jackson Pollock painting.

"Fuck! Goddammit, not here, not now. Fuck!"

Cambodia has a lot of things going for it, but in general, healthcare isn't one of them. The answer to the common question of;

"Well, whad'ya do if you get sick here?", has long been;

"Ya don't."

I hugged the walls of the hotel corridor and ambled towards the elevator and down to the street. Saturday night on Street 136 was in full Satyricon mode, with a cross between the *Stars Wars* cantina crowd and something out of *Blade Runner*. Normally it's a wonderfully heady and otherworldly mélange of humanity... if you're feeling well.

Pre-hospital care in a western sense doesn't really exist there, so I staggered over to a *tuk tuk*. That would not have been an uncommon sight for the drivers to have seen in general. Dizzy as hell with my continued exsanguination, I braced myself with both arms onto the metal crossbars and swayed to and fro, telling him that I needed to go to the Royal Phnom Penh Hospital. It was quite a drive, but really the only credible option. The driver smirked at me and said;

"Six dollars."

Again? It was my second experience of extortion at point of imminent death – and the same reaction,

'I'll die on this spot before accepting a tourist rate.'

I steadied myself, looked him square in the eyes and said;

"Five!"

"OK, get in."

A Saturday night emergency room admission at the top healthcare facility in the capital, with a full battery of tests and exams by a skilled and compassionate team ended with;

"Whatever happened has stopped. Nothing wrong with you now."

A couple of hundred bucks later, and I even caught the last set of the show.

> "And I just don't care what happens next
> Looks like freedom but it feels like death
> It's something in between, I guess
> It's Closing Time"
> *Leonard Cohen*

***

Taps

In 1981 I spent three months living at the Valley Forge Military Academy in Pennsylvania. I was twenty-four. I made friends with a nice, shy eighteen-year-old kid named Tom. There weren't a lot of other 'civilian' guys our age there, and in the way that water seeks its own level, we bonded with a few other kids, named; Tim, Evan and Sean.

It was good fun during the days, playing with guns and tanks, and if you had your moxie on, you'd be deigned an opportunity to play a game of chess with 'General Scott'. Nights were for drinking beer, going to the movies and flirting with the local town girls.

Was watching *Raiders of the Lost Ark* the other day, a film that I saw for the first time with Tom, Evan, and Tim, and was remembering just how young and fearless we all were back then. Tom outgrew his shyness and went on to fame and fortune in sixty other films to date since Taps. He wouldn't know me if he fell over me now. Older and wiser these days... well, definitely older... but... I've had a darned good run so far.

***

First love

"For god's sake Alvy, even Freud speaks of a latency period."
"Well, I never had a latency period. I can't help it."
W*oody Allen; Annie Hall*

Her name was Cindy. She had short blonde hair with tapered bangs. Her big blue eyes were the Sun, which lit up the million freckled stars that made up the rest of her face. She was my solar system.

I didn't know her well. I knew nothing of her dreams, goals or aspirations. I did know of her fears. Well one of them. It was a fear I regret exploiting to this day, but it was meant as a gesture of courtship. I brought over my favorite leopard frog to show her.

I was as impetuous then as I am now and didn't want to risk this one getting away so, in a moment of quixotic passion I invested my life savings on a diamond engagement ring to give her. I'd grabbed my entire twenty-five cent allowance without hesitation and pushed it into the slot. I pulled the B-7 lever and watched the ring drop into the tray below.

The next day I walked the three houses over and asked her to marry me. Her bright blue eyes marveled at the plastic stone. She said yes.

Our romance was brief, lasting but the afternoon before the serious business of skateboarding took over, but I never forgot her. Well maybe I did. But twenty years later, with my 'new' 1966 three-hundred-dollar Chrysler in New York City, I decided to cast Thomas Wolfe's advice aside and 'go home again'.

It was a good way to test my new wheels.

Driving across the Tappan Zee bridge to my old home, a drive that took a lifetime back when, but only forty-five minutes now, it all came rushing back. Everything did; the trees, the hiding places, the injury sites. But most of all, it was the freckles.

I knocked on the door of the house I'd once called home and had yelled 'Olly Olly oxen free' in front of. A place where I had once stashed my pet crayfish in the wax paper lining of a box of Captain Crunch cereal that I'd converted into a makeshift aquarium. A place whose dense forest of three poplar trees I knew like the back of my hand. The door opened a crack. A suspicious eye peered over the chain link of the secondary lock, and a woman tentatively said;

"Yes... may I help you?"

I enthusiastically stammered about how I'd lived right in this house so many years ago, and how very much I'd like to have a quick look around to... and then as I watched the chain shorten and disappear behind a door that quickly slammed shut, the folly of my innocence hit me, and I slinked away.

In for a penny, in for a pound. I continued down memory lane the three houses towards the last known residence of my seven-year-old childhood sweetheart. Feeling quite ridiculous at this point I soldiered on. I rang the doorbell and waited the eternity of half a minute before the door opened wide. Standing in the doorway, as preposterous as it could be, was a twenty-seven-year-old woman with blonde hair, a rumor of freckles and an incredibly welcoming smile.

"Hi, can I help you?"; she said.

With my heart in my throat I asked her if her name was Cindy?

She gave me that practical joke smirk people have and while looking over both of my shoulders, she let out a small giggle and said that she was. I said;

"Well, then technically... we're still engaged!"

She reflexively closed the door halfway before I reminded her of our brief romance and about the diamond ring. Cindy paused, regarding me in a distant way while flipping through her ancient Rolodex of experiences before flinging the door wide open and beaming;

"You're little Johnny Fengler??"

I don't think I'd ever turned a darker shade of embarrassed red in my life, before casting my eyes downward and timidly admitting that;

"Yes, that's me. I go by John now."

We talked for hours about things old and new and drank lemonade. And not the packaged nickel a glass stuff from the stand we used to sell from, but real lemonade.

She confessed to having missed me the whole summer I was, unbeknownst to her, in camp. She thought I'd run off with another girl. It was an all-boys camp I told her, as if that exonerated my disappearance.

As evening approached, I said that it was time for me to head back to the city. Neither of us wanted this strange re-alignment to end but both knew of course that it had to. We hugged like good old friends, strange in that we'd never even held hands before. And then as sudden and ridiculous as it could be, still in embrace, we made out in her living room, squeezing two lost decades into a single vigorous kiss.

It was an improbable moment of life synergy that she should be back home and alone at the exact moment I would choose to inexplicably reappear.

We both composed ourselves to say goodbye, silently acknowledging the flicker of time that had just passed between us, one which would become yet another multi-decade memory of something that happened so long ago.

***

A man needs a maid

I have a maid. She comes every two weeks and works non-stop for four hours. Washes my sheets, takes the blades out of my fans to dust them, folds my plastic supermarket bags into neat little triangles and pulls the hose up to the second floor to wash pigeon shit off the outside walls of the house. I pay her the exorbitant rate of $15 a visit. She's awesome.

Yesterday she informed me that she would only be coming once a month now. I asked why. She said;

"Because you not dirty enough for two times a month."

Oh, yeah. You want me dirty two times a month, do ya? Well do ya punk?

Reminded me of a one night stand I had... back when you could do that sort of thing. Think it was about 1976? Was a German woman in a club, a few years older than me. She wore tight black leather pants and I'm pretty sure she had a bullwhip in her closet.

In the morning she sat up, slipped her legs over the side of the bed, lit a cigarette, and without looking at me said in her sultry Marlene Dietrich voice;

"I cannot see you ever again."

I looked at her with my nineteen-year-old doe eyes and pleaded why.

She said; "Because you have no evil in you."

I was strangely offended.

'Do too. Wanna see?'

To date it was the most off-putting compliment I've ever received. Been trying to live it down for decades, to no avail.

***

Pretty Peaches

Finally got around to watching *The Deuce*, its' Times Square of the 70's felt like a home movie to me. But by the end of the decade I found myself in a film class in Northern California. I made friends with a strong, silent type of guy named Michael who I'd been paired up with to share equipment. He was smart, clean-cut, and 'religiously' polite.

One day after class he offered me a ride back to town in his car. The prospect of eight miles on my bicycle in blazing sun held little attraction so I locked it up and accepted. He drove a two-tone beige and brown El Dorado Cadillac.

"What the hell? We're college students, man. How in the world did you get this?"

We were shooting the breeze when he asked me what I'd done the night before. Without thinking I blurted out that I'd gone to the movies in nearby Petaluma.

They only had one theatre in town then and on Wednesdays they showed porn. This was a Thursday. He asked me what the movie was that I'd seen, as we were both film students it was a common topic. I panicked and stammered, not wanting to offend what I believed were his Christian sensibilities. Hoping to shake him off the trail, I said;

"Oh um, just some stupid thing. I don't remember."

He persisted.

"Come on, what was it?"

I mustered my courage and confessed. "OK, it was a porno."

"Huh, who was in it?"

"What're kidding me? I don't know. Some porn people."
"Well, was Desiree Cousteau in it?"
"What? How could you possibly... wow, she was, actually. Why would you even know that?"
"Well, I don't tell too many people this, John, but you seem trustworthy. I'm a porn star."
"Shut the fuck up. You are not."
"Ha, I am actually. Bet you didn't know that Petaluma is pretty much the porn capital of the world, did ya?"
"Well, well... how do you... how would I, no, I mean... how did you wind up doing that?"
"Pretty much the only qualification you need is to have a big dick. It's not brain surgery. I met some people and..."

We became fast friends for the rest of the semester, but I was never able to weasel my way into a shoot. Maybe I didn't qualify?

I never saw him again until about twenty years later as he was heading into a restaurant in San Francisco with what I took to be his wife. I recognized him immediately and with great enthusiasm shouted his name.

He reached back through time, scanned me up and down, darted his eyes quickly towards the woman he was with, and then back to me. He flashed a desperate and panicked plea of non-disclosure, much like a catcher shaking off a pitch.

I caught it immediately and gave the very slightest of nods, letting him know his secret was safe with me. I made a brief introduction as an old college pal and expressed my apologies for having to run off without time to catch up. I looked at his wife and smiled, before looking solemnly at him, concluding our brief reminiscence. I heard him audibly exhale in gratitude and relief as I walked past, as the last reel of our friendship in film flickered by announcing;
'The End'.

***

Monaco

I'd been invited by a Parisian friend to her family's flat in Monaco.

Several days in I decided to go all out, as one does in Monte Carlo. I figured I'd never get another chance, and why not go to a ridiculously high-end restaurant. It only had four or five tables, with weathered money patrons eviscerating me with their eyes, while deftly slipping bits of chateaubriand into the maws of their pocket pooches.

I can speak passable French in an emergency, and this was clearly an emergency. The maître d' respectfully presented me with a menu that was printed in Monegasque with gothic font. There were no prices next to the choices.

'If ya have to ask...'

I understood absolutely nothing on it.

My friend had declined my invite with something akin to;

"Don't be ridiculous, John, I'm from here. We don't go to places like that".

Reminds me of an *I Love Lucy* episode, where Lucy invites the Mertz's to a French restaurant. She proudly pointed to a spot on the menu and announced that;

"We'll have four orders of this!"

The waiter said;

"I'm very sorry Madame, but you cannot have that."

Lucy was indignant and said;

"I am the customer, I speak perfect French, and I want four orders of this!"

The waiter replied;

"Very well, Madame, four orders of 'closed on Tuesday'."

Channeling Lucy, I too pointed blindly, thinking;

'How wrong could it be?'

A short while later, my *rognons de veau* arrived. Veal kidneys. Rare veal kidneys... in a plate of blood.

I must have turned ghostly white as the maître d' slid over to my table to ask if everything was alright. I stammered that I'd made a mistake in my order, and...

"Oh, monsieur, if there is a problem..."

"No, I'm sure these are the finest raw veal kidneys in blood in the world. I just..."

And then the kind and knowing smirk of someone who'd seen through your charade all along, came to my rescue.

"Yes, I understand. Would Monsieur be happier with a beefsteak instead?"

Monsieur was very pleased, and even more so as the kidneys never found their way onto my bill.

***

Talkin' Turkey

...with a retired foreign correspondent last night got me thinking of a trip there a few years ago. My plane landed at the old Ataturk international in Istanbul at the exact same time as half a dozen other flights.

There were literally five to six hundred people queued up for only three open immigration windows. It seemed an interminable endeavor. A finagler since birth, as well as someone with a very short attention span, I frantically searched the hall for a fix to this untenable situation. There were about a dozen closed windows next to the three that were open. And then I spotted a small immigration window at the very far end of the hall that was lit up with no one in front of it. I walked the hundred feet over to it, only to see a sign that read;

"For citizens of Iraq only."

I looked back at the six hundred people in line, then at the 'Iraqi citizens only' line, and thought;

"Well hell, we pretty much bought the place anyway, so..."

I took out a twenty-dollar bill and slipped it through the window along with my US passport. The guy gave me half a smile, slipped the twenty out of sight, and slapped a visa stamp into my passport. Not a word spoken during the ten second process.

Merhaba!

***

Echo

Before there was Thailand, a million trillion years ago, there was Taiwan. I met a girl. We dated for a bit before I confronted her with something that had been on my mind. I said;

"I need to ask you... you galivant around town at clubs and restaurants, which is fortunate for me as that's how I met you, but... you seem to have a lot more money than a poor Chinese girl who works in a bank ought to?"

She cast her beautiful almond eyes downward and said;

"Oh, I think you leave me if I tell you."

I said;

"I think I leave you if you don't."

She steeled herself and confessed that she was a nude model on the side.

"For real artists you know... professionals. Nothing ugly, but not technically legal here. Is underground. They pay very well."

I broke out in a big smile and exclaimed;
"Really??"
"You not angry with me?"
"No, I'm a California boy. Can I do it too?"
"Oh my god, we would be so famous if we posed together. They never have interracial couple before."

And sure enough, we were the toast of the town for the next six months. I was even pulled aside after one of our first sessions by the woman who ran the studio, who said in perfect English;

"You know we like your body very much."

I was beaming and thanked her. And then she completed her thought with;

"Yes, not typical muscular American."

And so it goes...

***

Grand Central Sauna and Hot Tubs

There was an interregnum - a time between here and there, early eighties, when I became the night manager of... a place for relaxation by the hour. We didn't ask questions. Politicians, lawyers, junkies, jazz musicians, guys who had to 'work late' and working gals and guys... lots and lots of working folks.

My night staff included;

Bob, who had a punk band as his really late-night job called Bob Noxious and the Fuckups. He once took me to Mabuhay gardens in North Beach, back when punk was new and dragged me into a mosh pit... but I digress. One night a half dozen brothers descended the street level stairs to the bowels of Market Street and our subterranean San Francisco bath house with pantyhose over their faces. One guy came around the counter and stuck a .45 in my face. He told to open the register and lay down, which I did.

Another guy took out a Bowie knife and stuck it blade up between Bob's legs and marched him back to the rooms which he was forced to open so that they could rob the guests.

I was working up front that night with a girl named Shelly. She laid down as well, per instructions, but for some inexplicable reason, chose to do so on her back. The bad guys cleaned out the register, including the twenty-dollar bill that acted as the circuit breaker for the silent police alarm.

About two minutes after trying to shake ourselves off, after they split, I caught sight of a shotgun in the concave mirror on the stairway, as another half dozen well-armed guys rounded the corner and pointed weapons at our heads. They yelled at us to put our hands up. They had badges dangling from their plaid shirt 'plainclothes' outfits. I yelled back;
"Fuck, they already got the money. What the hell else do you want with us?"
"What?"
"The bad guys... they're long gone."
The head cop turned to Shelly and barked;
 "What did they look like?"
She stammered;
"They were long, black, and had a hole in the middle!"
"What the fuck are you talking about?"
"The gun!! That's all I saw!"

She'd been laying on her back looking up...
Not the first nor the last time I'd been held up at gun point in the Zen mecca of San Francisco. Just another 'relaxing' night in the urban jungle.

***

How suite it is...

Was looking at my pack of strawberry flavored condoms and the bottle of Cool mint Listerine in my Bangkok minibar a couple of years ago and remembered a trip to California a couple of years before that...
I'd booked a cheap room at a casino in Reno for the post forty-hour snooze. I arrived at the reservation desk mid-brouhaha with an outraged Iowan couple whose lifelong dream of an endless salad bar and penny slots was being upended by;

"I'm very sorry sir, but we don't have your booking in the system, and we just gave out the very last room we have."

The Iowans were apoplectic and litigious. I was on the ebb tide of exhaustion and leaned over to the Bell Captain.

"Hey, give them my room and stick me in a broom closet. I really don't care."

The Iowans had defused and departed, when the Bell Captain gave me a conspirator's nod and said;

"Actually we do have just one more room and know that this will never happen to you again in your life, but I'm grateful. The Honeymoon Suite is yours and thanks again."

"No really, it was no problem, but seriously I'm just gonna throw my day pack on the floor and crash for six hours. It'll be completely wasted on me. Just put me in a..."

"Really, sir, it is our only room. Enjoy."

And so I did.

***

The Mule

Luang Prabang in Laos is a UNESCO world heritage town. Considered by many to be the Paris of Asia, it's a pint-sized gem of a city, its waistline kept in place by the girdle of two rivers, the Mekong and the Nam Khan.

I've been chilling out there for years.

Laos as well as a few other spots in Southeast Asia benefit from what I call the spoils of war. The French left colonial architecture, as well as the recipes for coffee, breads and European service. It is replete with temples and monks and is regarded as a very holy and spiritual town. It also was home, until last year, to one of the most nostalgically outdated airports in the world, with refreshingly archaic disregard to process and security.

I have a favorite guesthouse as well as a favorite room, which is known to the owner and always made available to me as a frequent guest. He is a very nice and gentle Lao man, who seems to only exist for the pleasure of caring for his guests and never asks for a thing. Well almost never.

On the morning of my last departure, while settling my bill, the owner who I'd known casually for several years, mentioned that his sister now lived in Chiang Mai and ran a Laotian restaurant.

He asked if I would mind bringing back some special Lao curry for her.

"She'll meet you at the airport:)"

He then led me over to a corrugated box that was taped shut and tied with blue safety ribbon. It was about the size of an old Royal typewriter, or the packaging that would hold it.

"It's just 5 kilos," he reassured me.

I took an awkward inhale as I looked from the sealed package to his face.

Sensing my 'curiosity' he gently barked something in Lao to one of his staff, who then deftly slipped the blue ribbon and tape off and sprung back the lids to reveal 25 innocent baggies filled with a thick brown paste. A bouquet of curry did waft out as well.

5kgs of thick brown paste transported from one end of the Golden triangle to the other, with only one pesky international border and a one-hour flight between them.

His eyes registered satisfaction and he said that now I'd seen the contents no further reassurances would be needed.'

Blue ribbon and tape were re-attached as my friend asked if this was my final choice of attire before leaving, as he wanted to include my shirt color in the description he would give to his sister.

Non Compass Mentis

From under his desk he pulled out an old blue carry-on flight bag. It was the kind used by Pan Am flight attendants when Pan Am still existed, and stewardesses wore long white gloves and had Dippity Doo in their hair. It was the kind of bag that would be secreted away in a locker at JFK for six months until the heat was off and the loot, the jewels, the gold bars could be collected, if only the guy with the locker's key and number hadn't gotten pinched on an old warrant and wound up with an ice pick in him up in Sing Sing. He would die there but not before telling one of the guards he'd befriended, where the key was.

It was that kind of bag.

The sealed box was then slipped into the Pan Am bag and zippered closed. The guesthouse staff even carried the tote to the *tuk tuk* to lessen my burden still further. Uneven piles of unattended preflight luggage were stacked next to the harried yet unconcerned flight staff at the airport. I added my tagged bags to the mess and walked to the prop plane.

On the hour-long flight a niggling concern distracted my benevolent memories of my recent stay at my favorite guest house. How well did I really know my friend the owner? And what would be the street value of 5 kilograms of pure Lao opium?

'But I didn't know! I thought it was curry!'

Baggage claim belt number 3 in Chiang Mai on the first pass of my Pan Am bag, the handle slipped through my unexpectedly moist sweaty palm, and I had to chase it down the belt.

Now walking through the doors and out to the world, my vision narrowed by the fog of fear, my eyes locked with a smartly dressed woman who greeted me at twenty feet with a cautious but disarming smile. She unreassuringly glanced from side to side as she closed the last few paces between us.

In an effort to make some fledgling gesture of disassociation, I placed the bag on the tile floor between us, rather than the more overt and less awkward move of handing the bag right to her.

It was a legal loophole I hoped not to have to rely on, like the caveat where one can place medications on a neutral surface, where a patient may take them themselves, absolving the caregivers from the accusation of dispensing medication without a license.

Minimal pleasantries were exchanged as she leaned over to pick up her bounty. She gracefully pivoted on her sensible heels and slipped out to the world. But just before that I thought I read in her eyes,

'Very good, Son. Next run will be 20 kgs, and we'll go from there.

But the only part that really resonated with me was the 'run' part, which I did post-haste.

***

Medialuna

There's a crescent moon tonight. Made me immediately think about the croissant-like pastries of Argentina. Was flirting with Buenos Aires as a final resting place a decade and a half or so ago. I'd taken three months of tango lessons which I thought more than justified a look see.

Milonga's, steak and a bottle of Malbec every night for a month. It was delightful.

Decided one day to venture over to Uruguay, which was about an hour's ferry ride across the bay.

I got through customs and almost through immigration, when an overly stern officer started dressing me down and slapping my passport, trying to indicate a missing document.

I was unceremoniously escorted to a private room where a female immigration officer informed me of my gross and costly breach of procedures. I protested of course, having full confidence in my case. We went back and forth on this for a bit when a light went off in my head. I immediately relaxed and smiled, remembering that I was in South America, and that this was nothing more than a common shakedown.

I smiled and said;
"How much?"
She tersely replied;
"Forty dollars, señor."
Now fully on my turf I said;
"Thirty!"
She agreed. As it was, I only had two twenties which I handed over to her. She smiled, reached into her own purse and pulled out a ten for change and told me to enjoy her country.

Continuing my crime spree, I decided to try Uruguayan steak and a bottle of Malbec.

My bill came. It said; $935. I completely freaked out before coming to my senses and remembering that the Argentine exchange rate was 4:1 US.

I relaxed for a moment before freaking out again on a still exorbitant $235 dinner bill. And then some kindly patron who saw the look of panic on my face informed me that Uruguay's exchange rate was 35:1 US. Ah, a $26 meal after all.

The next day I decided to go up the Uruguay River on a local boat. I went down to the pier and bought a round trip ticket and settled in between a cage of chickens and a winter's worth pile of charcoal.

It was a stunning ride, with people exiting at various unmarked spots to carry their goods through the jungle to their villages.

Several hours in, I realized I was the only passenger left. Cool.

The captain sitting comfortably with one hand on the wheel, his other cradling his maté cup. At one point he turned around and did an astonishing double-take at seeing me.

"*Donde va, señor?*"

He wanted to know where I was going. I said I had no idea,

"But I have a return ticket right here."

I proudly said. Registering a bit of alarm he switched to English and said;

"But I no go back."

I said;

"Ever??"

"Not today, señor."

So he dropped me at some wooden jetty somewhere deep in the pampas, as we'd left the main river ages ago. He said;

"Wait here and maybe someone will be going back."

"Maybe??"

And there I was, standing on a rickety jetty; snakes, alligators, capybaras - God knows what.

About thirty minutes later, more than improbably, a diminutive barefoot Frenchman appeared. He said he was in charge of the entire biosphere that I was in now, where he served as liaison between government, villagers and rebel groups.

"You are lucky that I knew you were here."

"How did you know actually?"

"I live in the jungle. You are from the city. There are different smells, different sounds. We just know."

We chatted for hours at a nearby hut he walked me to. We drank tea and talked about snake anti-venom, which he had to go for twice yearly at the university in Montevideo to replace the expired one that was kept in a central box equidistant from all the local villagers. We spoke about politics, sustainability and about snuggling with capybaras. Must be some long nights out there. Was an extraordinary afternoon. And then he stopped and said;

"Oh, your boat is coming."

"But I don't hear anything."

"No, you wouldn't."

We walked back to the jetty where he reached over and took out a long wooden pole that had a piece of white material attached to it. He leaned it out over the tributary, which I took to be the local sign for a passenger pick up.

Sure enough, several minutes later, a small boat with a single family pulled up. My biosphere pal bid me adieu and I boarded. I proudly pulled out my return ticket to show them. They looked terribly confused and turned back to the task at hand of returning me to the world.

**

Evaluations

We were called to one of the outer districts of San Francisco for the vague, one size fits all; 'eval', which could be anything from a shooting;

"Oh, it's only a small hole, so I didn't tell the dispatcher", to a mummified corpse that had been decomposing for three months under a bush in the park.

"We thought he was just sleeping."

'Evals' were the Forrest Gump of medical calls.

They were the box of chocolates where you never knew what you were gonna get, but you were pretty sure each piece was gonna have some lice on it. Arrived at the door and greeted by a weary old woman with;

"Oy, I'm so glad you're here. It's the Alzheimer's. I can't handle him anymore."

I gave her a compassionate look and asked where her husband was.

"He's in the back bedroom."

"OK ma'am, my partner is gonna ask you a few questions while I go check out your husband."

As I entered the bedroom I was solemnly greeted by an elderly man with;

"Thank God you're here. It's the Alzheimer's again. You've got to take her in."

"Wait, what??"

Or take the case of Mary and Joseph; he a naked, razor thin seventy-five-year-old bag of bones covered in wilting black skin, bound to his bed frame in four-point restraint, his corpulent Irish wife on the adjacent bed who was wailing;

"I can't breathe, I can't breathe, I can't breathe, I can't breathe... "

"Ma'am, you just said that seven times. You're breathing fine. Why are we really here? And why is your husband naked and tied to his bed."

As I began to untie Joseph, considering that no possible explanation would justify his further humiliation, she gave me a 'damn you for seeing through my ruse' look and said;

"Well alright then. It's his masturbatin'. He just won't stop, and it gets everywhere. I just can't take it anymore."

About twenty minutes later a Social Worker arrived with a thick case file under her arm and told me that;
"Yes, it's true. He's a chronic masturbator. I've been dealing with them for a while."
"That's nice. We'll just leave him in your hands then... as it were."
And off to the blocked storefront in the financial district for the inebriated;
"Ssaaam... I am."
"OK, Sam I am, which hospital would you like to have lunch at today?"
Just then a lurking citizen announced himself, complaining that;
"This man is one of God's creatures and deserves the same amount of respect as everyone else!"
And in the 'timing is everything' way that a perfect life can be sometimes, I turned to Mr. Citizen and said;
"Well it appears that one of God's creatures is urinating on your loafers right now."
He looked down in horror and scurried away, leaving us with Sam and his deviously satisfied grin that I briefly shared in a strangely complicit way. And each day would rattle and hum with a dozen other stories like this, for weeks, months, and years on end, with you developing that nascent belief that somewhere down the road, you too will wind up being just another 'eval' in another medic's future story.

***

Fine, and you?

An errant spark from a passing cigarette on Sukhumvit a few years ago landed on my hand. It caused me to drop my coffee cup in front of a policeman and a prostitute.

The cop in a quick draw, whipped out his littering fine book. As I leaned down to pick up my cup I asked;

"How much?"

The girl was quicker on the draw this time and said, "2,000 baht."

The cop laughed and said;

"Yes, that correct. Littering is 2,000 baht fine."

She shot the cop a competitive look.

Realizing it was a zero-sum game, we all laughed and bid each other a good day.

***

Dry County

Just realized that my dad, improbably, would have been 93 today. How is that possible? And then I remembered how old I was. Jeez.

Father's Day

I laid my dad to rest on Father's Day. Timing is everything.

He was born in what was soon to become East Germany, passed away in Florida and, for reasons that are still unclear to me, was buried in Kentucky.

We took the same flight together from Fort Lauderdale to Nashville, and I'll never forget watching his casket de-plane down the cargo ramp while I was queued up to exit the plane. Many eyes were transfixed on the 'luggage' belt, with those nearest to me making nervous comments like;

"Wonder what the in-flight entertainment was like down there for that guy?"

If my dad had been alive, he would've been laughing along with them. The traveling funeral circus continued with a four-hour drive to rural Kentucky, where I checked into a local hotel and immediately asked where the closest liquor store was. The reception gal smiled at me and said;

"That'd be in Tennessee, darlin'."

I said;

"Yeah, that's funny, no, but seriously?"

She said;

"Honey, I am serious. This here's a dry county."

I stammered that this was the birthplace of bourbon, and;

"How could that be??"

She tried to placate me with;

"Not this part of Kentucky, but fortunately the border's only fifteen minutes away."

So back to Tennessee I went, girding myself for the disconcertingly foreign Southern Baptist onslaught of my stepmom's clan that was to follow the next day.

Happy birthday, Dad

***

Dusit Thani

I had a friend who managed an iconic hotel in Bangkok that I used to frequent. I hadn't seen him in a few years. He inquired about my absence, to which I confessed my hotel infidelity. He smiled and said;

"Ah, she's an old dame now. One has to come to expect things like that."

John Fengler

The Dusit Thani hotel in Bangkok is another 'old dame', opened in '69. It was a sad day when they announced it would be closed, to be replaced by another soulless urban monolith. I've resurrected one of my favorite memories of the Dusit to commemorate its closure.

***

Plus ça change, plus c'est la même chose
Dateline: U.S. Embassy, Bangkok, 1983

I was so starved for something to read in English that I ambled down to my local embassy for a copy of *Stars and Stripes* magazine. Whoever thought that the Reagan era would've been considered 'simpler times', but they were. At least less cumbersome re: embassy access and commissary hall passes. It used to be a lovely place to while away the afternoon truth be told, with verdant gardens, neo-Colonial architecture, a welcome smile from the staff and best of all, free A/C.

Access was as simple as walking up to the Marine on sentry duty, flashing your passport and getting a laminated visitor's pass which was to be affixed with an alligator clip onto your t-shirt. I was walking around the compound, peeking here and poking there when I spotted a girl, or should I say, she spotted me? Her name was Anna. She was there to authenticate her pet parrot. I was fascinated by her Latin frame, her fiery eyes, as well as the concept of getting a bird visa.

Our flirtation was nearing its natural limits as I followed her from room to room, watching as she got this and that waiver and stamp. We had both run out of reasons to linger. It was that awkward segway period between acceptance and rejection. Someone had to flinch.

"Well, I'm off to the Department of Forestry next. ... It was nice meeting you."

"Um, yeah... really nice."
"You could come along if you like?"
"Really? I'd love to."
"Great. Ya know my mom works here, so we can just get a staff car and a driver."

So out the front door of the embassy and into a waiting staff car we went. We really hit it off, and in an uncharacteristically bold way I suggested we meet for an evening on the town. We agreed to meet at Lumpini park by the statue.

"Everyone knows it."

We met and strolled around a bit before stumbling into the Dusit Thani hotel. I didn't know how many stars it garnered, but I was pretty sure there were no backpackers staying there, so it was already above my pay grade. We coursed the lobby following the disco sound until finding the entrance. I watched couple after couple walk to the front, sign a piece of paper and walk in. I said;

"Come on let's see if we can get in."

I asked the gal at reception if we too could sign and go in?

"Sure", she replied. "Just write your name and room number and have a good time."

Feeling confident I went to the bar and said;
"Hey, can we sign for drinks too?"
"Of course you can." Same deal as before.

Well this was working out fine. I was getting hammered in a disco, with free booze and great prospects of a new female friend who didn't charge. Everything was going well until suddenly, the light around us darkened. I broke from my wild gyrations on the dance floor to see that we were surrounded by gun wielding hotel security who were wearing tight fitting brown uniforms just like the police.

A tepidly polite man in a business suit stepped into the middle of the circle that was now around us on the dance floor.

He pulled a clip board out with the sign in sheets on it and addressed us in the way people of authority do, who already know the answer to their question but err on the side of decorum;

"This is you write name? We have not this room."

"Oh, oh yeah, sorry. It's really... 2901."

"Yes, sir. We also don't have this room too."

I caught Anna's drunken eyes for a moment, switched into some rapid extrication speech, something to do with our parents having booked this family trip and there was some confusion... and then I just grabbed Anna's arm and yelled;

"RUN."

We both shot off in the same direction. We'd made it about eight feet when we were cornered and remanded to a makeshift 'disco jail', walled in by glitter balls, velvet ropes and nervous security guards with hands on their holsters. We were ordered to pay our now exorbitant bill right then. This was a place where drink prices were slightly more than a night's rent. We just didn't have it.

My new girlfriend of six hours said;

"It's O.K. I'll go to the embassy and borrow it from my mom."

I said I was concerned that the embassy might not want to be involved in a local police matter involving a staff member's daughter and some random backpacker, as well it was now nighttime. Anna shuffled her feet a little and replied;

"She um, works on the second floor", whatever the hell that meant, but seemed to imply a broader reach, an imperiality, and most importantly late hours. The effect was marginally reassuring. I was relying on her honesty and integrity to not leave me in disco custody forever.

A couple of long hours later she showed up with a huge smile and a wad of cash. She bailed us out and even gave the waitresses a tip which they begrudgingly accepted.

We ran back to the park like little kids who had just robbed the candy store. I thanked Anna for a lovely evening and invited her for breakfast.

"Sure," she said.

I smiled;

"Shall I call you... or nudge you."

We got along well. As well as two people between life stations and no plans for their lives past the month could. For her part she had a couple of weeks left before she and her parrot were due back at university. A couple of weeks was a lifetime back then. I suggested the beach. All bamboo hut lodging, no electricity or water... on me!

It was to be Koh Samet, which for those who know of it now and couldn't possibly imagine it in its more primitive incarnation, was paradise. We spent two weeks doing what new lovers with no responsibility on a tropical beach do. Sometimes we left the hut.

Bussing back to Bangkok at the end of our affair, with heartfelt promises to stay in touch, we arrived exactly where we had met; the U.S. Embassy.

She dropped me off at the front, kissed me goodbye, and continued to the back entrance that was relegated to employees of 'the second floor.' I lingered for a few moments before strolling up to the Marine sentry of the day, who was red faced in the Bangkok heat to begin with as he leaned out of his guard house.

"Can I help you, sir?", he asked.

I fished around my backpack for my passport and my fingers closed around an object I'd totally forgotten about. It was my laminated, alligator clipped visitor's pass. I pulled it out with a self-satisfied smile and handed it to him saying;

"Oh yeah, I never turned this in. Here ya go."

I'd never witnessed such a dramatic and barely controlled turn to rage in my life. He was vibrating with anger, neck muscles distended, teeth set almost to cracking point.

"YOU MISERABLE LITTLE FUCK! Do you know we put this entire embassy on red alert because of you? We locked down because you didn't turn in your pass, and we had an unaccounted-for visitor still on the grounds."

He was seething. I tepidly smiled and said;

"Hey, I left in an embassy staff car. Guess you gotta do something about your security procedures here pal."

Yes, I did call a well-armed and enraged Marine; 'Pal'. Probably wouldn't do it again, but times have changed.

I think he realized the implications to his job description, combined with the relative immunity a naive backpacker brought to the situation. He snatched the pass, told me NEVER to darken his doorway again not to even think of coming in for another copy of *Stars and Stripes*!"

Ironically, I would see him again soon enough as I arrived on time for my own job interview. Through clenched teeth and glaring uncomprehending eyes, he hissed;

"Here's your new pass, sssir. Please follow me."

I never heard from Anna again.

***

Omi

I went to my grandmother's ninetieth birthday party in NY a bunch of years ago. She took her leave from the festivities early and I helped her to bed. I sat for a minute talking to her before broaching an awkward topic. She was raised in a world of German stoicism where many personal issues were just not discussed. I knew she was approaching her end of days and gingerly brought up the question of her remains. I said;

"Omi, you know no one lives forever, and... well, nobody knows what you would like done with your body after you pass?"

She sat there quiet and expressionless, so I nervously pressed on with;

"Would you like to be buried, or cremated, or..."

She deflated thoughtfully back into her propped-up pillow, looked me in the eyes, gave me the patented family smirk and said in her undiminished German accent;

"Surprise me."

***

All That's Holey

Was just prodded to remember an old friend who passed a while ago, 'on this day'. And so I do.

"Shall I introduce you as Father Thomas?"

"Oh Lord, no! Just plain ole' Tom is fine."

A humble Jesuit, happy to accept the bequeathed Cadillac here, the unused mountain home there but left to his own devices would hike with his orphaned Labrador and his pagan pal while wearing punctured tennis shoes;

"Well, I am a 'hole-y' man, no?!"

So pleased with his own jokes, as he should have been.

"Why? Because the FBI left me with too many questions and the seminary gave me the answers. Not all of them but enough."

"And so Tom, I'll posit to you the one question that has plagued me, that I'm sorry to say will continue to plague me no matter what you come up with. If everything is forgivable, where is accountability?"

"Well maybe that's the difference between occupations. One offered judgement, the other mixes in forgiveness. They're not mutually exclusive you know.

And chastity since I know you'll ask... again.... yeah, I'm still a guy and have tasted, lived in the 'real' world but, well hell, sure we all make sacrifices.

I tend to my flock, offer something short of salvation to grateful people and in my spare time live my imperfect life.

And I'm blessed to be able to hang out with you on my sabbaticals. I have my orphan dog and my good health. And yet despite our differences here we are, both soaking in the same beauty of this desolate mountain. And I know you have the good beer for when we get back.

I'm still mortal after all."

Yes, you are my good friend. RIP Father Tom, wherever your divergent beliefs have you resting.

***

The Fingahs

My dad was a *Mad Man.* In 1960 he got the Chrysler account. He went off to Detroit for a shoot and found himself gazing down the décolletage of the diaphanous gowned model who was draped over the hood of the display car. She was 'Miss Chrysler, 1960'. Shortly after that she became my stepmom.

My dad used to take me on the set when I was a kid and, naturally I'd go hang out around the models. They were broken down into body parts, self-identifying with;

"Oh, I'm legs.",

'Oh, I'm lips',

"Oh, I'm, well you're too young for me to tell you what my best feature is, but..." and then she'd wink and shimmy her chest.

To this day I can't watch a smiling spokeswoman on a commercial, holding up whatever she's trying to sell, without imagining the hand model kneeling in front of her and lifting up her arms where the face model's arms would be, had she also been graced with perfect hands.

My stepmom had perfect hands and went on to fame and fortune letting her "fingers do the walking through the Yellow Pages". Wonder who under forty even knows what the Yellow Pages were? I wonder how strongmen demonstrate their strength now. Ripping an iPhone in half seems less of a challenge.

Shortly after my mom was informed that Mexico hadn't required her presence for a legally binding divorce in California, she began a lifelong descent into bitterness. She spent the next five and a half decades asking any and all for updates on 'the fingahs', which was how she referred to her replacement who had gone from Chrysler to the Yellow Pages.

My mom, who could famously make a sailor blush, once applied for a job as an executive secretary. During the interview she became impatient and said;

"Listen, do I get the job or not?

The interviewer replied;

"Well Madame, you don't have enough of what we call, savoir faire."

She leaned forward and growled;

"I'll tell ya, Mack, at this point I don't have enough subway fare."

Mom and Dad are now long passed but the 'fingahs' thrives at ninety. Happy birthday to Miss Chrysler, 1960.

**

The Twelve hours of Christmas

We were called to a squalid downtown tenement late one Christmas Eve. It was for the;

"Unknown. Crying kid. Advise if you need police."

It was the fourth floor of a six-story walk up. A dozen shattered dreams to a floor. The sticky hallway carpet was stained by dragged heels, ash, semen and neglect. A plaintive muffled cry emanated through the plywood door of room 402. No response despite repeatedly louder and more assertive taps, then knocks, then raps of a flashlight. A quick nod of agreement with my partner, then a strong-armed shoulder which splintered the doorframe.

The scene just beyond, an hour before Christmas proper, was of a blue and white striped sheet-less prison mattress, a motionless mid-thirties woman, syringe in hand, in arm, a freeze frame of tragedy lay mottled blue on top.

Not even acknowledging our abrupt entry, a four-year-old girl in a faded white nightdress stood purring tears over her unresponsive mother. And behind her, mockingly, the television tuned timelessly to the eternal flame of the yule log channel blazed on.

Police summoned to officially rule out a crime scene, which it clearly wasn't, crimes of inequity and circumstance notwithstanding. Child Protective Services called to usher in another victim in the cycle of poverty, despair and desperation, and an hour to go till end of shift.

Between divorces I had been given sanctuary at a childhood friend's home who had hit the Silicon Valley lotto. I slipped into their perfect penthouse loft, careful not to disturb. It was lit only by the kilowatt of Christmas lights that adorned their nine-foot tree. The lower half of the lights were blocked and diffused by the mound of professionally wrapped gifts that had only hours left before the massacre of Christmas morning.

Morning arrived through the fog of memory that daylight brings and washed away all but the soul crushing residue of last night's sadness.

The irony was stark as their Montesorri four-year-old stumbled out of her room wearing a non-faded white nightdress. She rubbed the sleep out of both eyes, then registered a small surprise to see me at the counter with mom and dad, then slowly looked around.

She began to vibrate as a distant tremor would, that in moments would create a tsunami. Her eyes bulged, her whole body taught with excitement, a silent scream before locking eyes onto the tree and then exploding with glee as the epiphany of Christmas hit her with full force.

Blazing a full tilt sprint to the pile of gifts, the majority of which of course were for her, she was the embodiment of privilege and joy.

And then the bile of memory hit me hard and soured my frozen smile which resembled the look you'd have when you're chatting at a party and you realize you've eaten something that needs to be discreetly ejected into a tissue, but you don't want to alert this to anyone, and there are no tissues in sight.

My friends of course oblivious to the world that gives shadow to their light, see my chagrin and cajole me to;

"C'mon, enjoy. It's Christmas."

The irony and sadness consume me, and I regret my resentment of my friend's daughter's happiness as I realize the grotesque disparity room 402's child was experiencing at the same moment. Swallowing yet another bite of angst I took my leave to head for the turnaround day shift that allowed a colleague to try and have a 'normal' life with his own family. Hey, it was double time.

Barely 8:30 a.m. on a sleepy Christmas morning someone forgot to tighten the lug nuts on a Chevy. The driver who was coming home or heading off to who knows where, his front left tire completely separated from the vehicle and rolled off at a 45-mph tangent. It continued until hitting the median that separated northbound traffic from south.

It then launched into the air and sailed full force until exploding through the multiple plate glass windows of a donut shop across the street, finally crashing to a rest upon the display counter inside, leaving a hemorrhage of jelly and blood stains on every surface.

An elderly couple had been among the displaced patrons. They had been sipping dishwater coffee that had been dunked with crullers. The tire had ripped through them and their windows and had sent a hurricane of glass shards through their faces and bodies which lay writhing on the floor.

My first emotion after arriving on the scene was the consummate sadness of an elderly couple spending Christmas morning in a donut shop on a quiet San Francisco boulevard.

My partner and I silently assessed and divided patients, as is the nature of our rescue language.

I went to the man, maybe eighty years old, his face a Cubist patchwork of flesh, blood and lacerations. His airway partially occluded by donut and lip. He looked at me selflessly, lovingly, and sputtered,

"My wife, she is OK?".

Oh my god, Immigrants!

My conceit and arrogance masked as compassion, it had never occurred to me that a quiet coffee and donut in a window on Christmas morning, having not perished in a death camp in German occupied Poland years before was in itself Christmas! Packing up our patients, my partner grabbed ahold of the shell-shocked kid behind the counter, pointed to the one intact display case and dead panned;

"We'll need a dozen jellies and a couple of bear claws... it's a crime scene ya know... evidence."

And not an hour later in the lull that Christmas morning usually provides, we too fell back into the quiet moments, dunking our ill-gotten pastries into Styrofoam cups of coffee, waiting for someone else's worst day of their lives.

***

Popeye

Few years ago I asked a Thai friend what her thoughts were re: a certain "someone" at the time;
"She nice, but fuckadee."
"What?"
"I say she have fuckadee."
"Spell it."
"F-A-C-A-D-E. Fuckadee!"
Tonight I was out to dinner with 'er indoors' when she ordered the fish;
"But change potato for pop I."
"What?"
"I don't know in English, but what 'pop I' eat."
"Spinach?"
"Yes."
Never a dull moment.

***

Riel life

Sopha leans imploringly over the bar, her breasts flattening across the oak counter as she pleads across a sea of western suitors. She hails over the din of the crowd;
"I need real someone!"
Leonard from Mustard upon Tweed, whose wife of 36 years left him 6 months ago for her yoga instructor, pops his head up from his Angkor beer and gives a body wag, like a tethered pup outside a shopping mall every time someone exits in hopes it's their owner. He leers over to her direction, affects a sardonic smile and sincerely professes his durability.
'I am a real someone' (choose me, choose me).
She shouts again, a little more desperate this time and directed past Leonard's face;

"I need real someone", then furrows her brow at her plea that goes unanswered. Sopha then waves a hunk of cash over her head at the crowded bar, as the mélange of expats slowly come to their collective epiphanies after doing the linguistic dance that is usually second nature earlier in the evening.

Leonard's head drops back down to his beer again with the force of a hanged man. Riel is the currency of Cambodia, but generally trade is conducted with U.S. cash and most of that is done with the highly coveted $1 bill.
Sopha's register almost dry, she needs some change, she needs some Riel and some one's.

***

The Buck stops here

Who knows how these memories get triggered but... back when the world was a bit more sane, I always traveled with my 'lucky' Buck knife. Bought it in junior high and have it to this day. I was going through airport security in Oakland, California and was pulled out by a diminutive agent. I'm talkin' real Snow White stuff. He opened my blade and placed it against the palm of his hand and announced that;
"I'm sorry, but FAA regulations stipulate that a knife blade cannot be longer than palm length."
I weighed my response for a moment before saying;
"Nothing personal, man, but c'mon... could I speak to someone with an adult sized hand?"
He stared me down, then gave half a smirk.
I was cleared to go.

***

The Major

Just revisited a post from 5 years ago about a man I met, and spent the evening with, at the Writer's Club in Chiang Mai. He was 91 at the time. This week he turned 96.

Sunday roast with my friend 'Major' Roy Hudson, who first came to Thailand as part of the British Territorial Army at the age of 28... 68 years ago.

"Landing in Cox's Bazar, in Bangladesh -well technically Bengal, East India at the time."

'So what brings you to my table at 91 years old, sir?

'"Oh my dear boy", he preened, mischief glinting through cataracts, "I am the doyen of this place, and I am happy to be graced by your presence at MY table."

"In fact if I were less of a gentleman and frankly less feeble, I would reclaim the seat I've been in for the past 50 years that you are enjoying now. As to your question regarding what brings me here, well I should say that the Royal British Engineers in 1942 did.

Wasn't here all that time mind you - spent a bit of it being pushed across Burma by the Japanese, escaping into Bangladesh. Managed to push the plunger a few times on the way though... And now I see that my chauffeur is here - Chiang Mai rules though; pie and ice cream are on me, the drinks are on you."

Happy birthday, Major.

***

Catamarooned

I first visited Pattaya in 1983, invited by a friend to go sailing at the Yacht Club.

The non-yacht club part of town that has lived in infamy lo these many years, was awful back then, consisting of too many dodgy people sitting in too many thatched roof bars, and I swore never to go back. That was thirty-six years ago, and yet here I am breaking my own promise.

The dodgy thatched roof bars are gone, replaced by an ocean of steel and concrete discos, but the memories linger... I'd been invited by a friend who knew this guy "who knows all about sailing, man".

"So what do those black flags on the beach mean?"

"Oh those are small craft advisories, man. But don't worry, they don't apply to catamarans. These are made for wind."

"Cool."

Non Compass Mentis

It was a sixteen-footer, and we were three people on it. It was designed to be the cliche three-hour tour. I remember making a bunch of sandwiches to take to the island we had intended to go to.

I had never been on a 'cat' in the ocean before and didn't know that there was zero storage on them, so I tied the baggies to the base of the mast and smiled in self-satisfaction. I was told to jump on, which was more literal than I'd expected, as we whooshed offshore in the blink of an eye. It was indeed dark, and it was stormy. We were in significant swells and out of the sight of land within minutes.

It was thrilling, and the captain was the most confident and enthusiastic guy I'd ever met. The drama of the seas increased, as did the size of the swells. Soon we were in dips so deep that they eclipsed everything save for the vertical walls of water around us.

And then we turtled.

Turtling is what happens when your craft becomes inverted, with the mast that had been pointing towards the open sky, now directing us towards a watery hell. One of the waves had plummeted down onto the bow tip and pushed us up into the air where we hovered, suspended until coming down on the wrong side. In a lake this would be an easy fix, using the weight and balance of the crew to cantilever the craft upright again. In a deep ocean swell with arrhythmic and unremitting crashes, not so much.

The trick was to go into the water and have the three of us push the 'cat' around until we were in position to have another enormous wave crash down and re-invert us again. This we did for six hours, our captain's indefatigable enthusiasm never wavering. Each time we would hit a Sisyphean wave which would pitch us almost vertical, several times going all the way up on a sixteen-foot wave, which had the three of us huddled at the tip of our sixteen-foot craft. We were suspended for a brief eternity thirty-two feet in the air, waiting to see which way we would bang down.

The first hints of dusk were starting to show, when finally our captain said;

"OK, we'll try a couple of more times, and if no luck we'll pull the sail up off the mast, wrap ourselves in it and wait till tomorrow."

"WHAT???? Tomorrow?? No! There's no fucking tomorrow in this story! Are ya kidding me?"

We caught the right wave a short time later and flipped back upright, but for how long? I had been in the water for hours. We all had. I was the one guy though that had put on a vest as I'd had a near drowning years earlier so was gun shy. We all congratulated each other, and only then did I confess my fear of drowning out there. The captain gave me a wry look and said;

"Really, I would have thought you would have been more nervous about the sharks. I was."

"WHAT??"

We turned into the wind and shot back to shore and were greeted by a furious yacht club staff who had reported us lost. The true miracle of this tale were the sandwiches, which had been submerged at the mast base all day in their little baggies. They were completely dry and delicious.

***

A rumor of tuna

I had a homeopathic tuna sandwich today - in that they believe that the smallest dose, dilution to the molecule, will build your resistance to whatever ails you. I had a hankering for tuna. If true, I am now immune.

It was a perfectly dry martini tuna sandwich, if the bread were gin, and the tuna were vermouth.

There was a whisper of tuna, as if angels were chatting about the secrets of the universe lest they be overheard.

There was an unseasonal dusting of tuna, much as the light crystalline snow will fall around you but evaporates the moment it hits the ground.

It was an air kiss of a tuna sandwich, catching the scent of a freshly washed cheek as pleasantries are exchanged.

It seemed as if there were, but one tuna left in the world, and it had to supply every sandwich for all eternity.

It was a chimera of a tuna sandwich - at once thinking you caught a of glimpse of it and then questioning your own sanity.

It was the moment at dusk tuna sandwich when you can no longer distinguish between a white thread and a black one.

It was the eye's pupil of a tuna sandwich -a potential space masquerading as an object.

It was the Marcel Marceau tuna sandwich, silently mocking me, miming a giant guffaw while holding its belly.

And yet after eating it, I was full. Filled with disbelief, remorse, and hunger.

***

Demons

"Oh, the things I've seen through your eyes."

It's taken me many years to re-discover the absolute magic of San Francisco, a town I had loved and called home for decades. To be able to hear the foghorn and not the siren. To feel the bracing grip of the marine layer that's replaced the choke hold of gang suppression. Letting the full inhale of eucalyptus supplant the rust of blood and the rot of bodily decay.

My guard is down. As much as a lifetime of inner-city wariness can let you drop it.

I see the fog enshrouded Golden Gate Bridge without instinctively looking for the 'floater' below it, without imagining a northbound approach via the southbound lanes for the "mid-span crash, multiple vehicles involved, reports of fatalities".

I imagine the room.

Above the Italian deli is filled with Silicon Valley executives, not the crushingly lonely and fearful immigrants from Eastern Europe or Central America for whom seeing a guy in a government uniform, despite best intention, is not a good thing. Where have they all been moved to?

I see a bustling downtown corner, filled with day trippers trying not to fall over their shopping bags, not the chalk outline around the crumpled body of a defenestrated twenty-year old Chinese girl.

I see the entrance to the best Carne Asada burrito shop in town, able to peer past the clouds of memories of the double stabbing "send backup now. Perp still on-scene".

I look up into the windows of apartment buildings and see Victorian soffits and not the dangling electric cord that snapped from the weight of the guy who'd been swinging from it.

I see the new blooms in the Arboretum, not the skeletal remains of a homeless man who had remarkably gone unnoticed for so long. To be invisible again, not the savior on a good day or the 'punk ass motherfucker' on a bad one.

Vanquished is the sadness I'd feel watching an elderly couple strolling hand in hand through North Beach, knowing that soon one of them will wake up and one will not. And gone too is my entomologist's eye as I pass the cardboard shelters of the lice covered homeless who are loudly railing against their schizophrenic gods. I don't look for the symmetrical burns on the hands of abused children, instead only hearing the laughter of youth.

And no longer do I wonder why my partner and I are the only ones wearing Kevlar vests on a sunny day at a concert in the park.

I have reclaimed my town.

It is good to be free of one's demons.

***

Alobar

About a dozen years or so ago, my best friend tripped on a piece of barbed wire while chasing a squirrel. He limped back home with a sad and guilty look that I'm sure was more pain than anything else.

I lived in a rural mountain home, which on a good day was a fair drive to healthcare. This was not a good day. This was a Saturday. And it was 'the' Saturday of the annual rural veterinary dinner that was being held in some far-off town. They were all in attendance. Turns out my little guy had an arterial bleed in his paw. I applied the best pressure I could with what I had at hand, but this injury needed surgical intervention now.

I was about twenty minutes from the nearest small town, deer and highway patrol notwithstanding, but the only real treatment option was in Reno, Nevada, which was a two-hour night drive away.

As I pulled into the nearest town, I looked in the backseat to see my little buddy sitting in a pool of blood. He was not gonna make the rest of the drive, so I decided to call in a favor.

I shot over to the local hospital, where I was known, hoping to be given a professional courtesy and a bunch of pressure bandages. I walked in to the E.R. looking like an extra from a Friday the 13th movie, covered in my dog's blood.

My unflappable colleagues looked up and asked what was going on. With minimally controlled agitation I recounted my dog's ordeal and solemnly told of the long drive ahead. And then a miracle happened. The biggest dog lover in the world just happened to be on duty that day.

The attending physician, a bald and bear sized Ukrainian, who had not yet turned around from his charts, suddenly slapped his hand on his desk, stood up, spun around and said;

"Dog don't go to Reno. Put dog on gurney and bring in here."

The medics, nurses and patients all froze. He scanned the room before continuing with;

"Anyone have problem with that?"

And into 'Trauma 1' he was rolled. Truth be known, they only had one room. At this point everyone was fully engaged and rallying my little guy, aiming the surgical boom light, making a sterile field, and keeping 'family' calm.

With him now sutured up and recovering, I let out a giant whimper of gratitude.

I said that I'd be writing the best, most heartfelt letter to the hospital administration, recounting in detail the tremendous kindness and professionalism of everyone who'd been on duty tonight.

Just then a panicked plea came out in unison; "NO! No letter! This never happened!!

Oh yeah, I forgot. A case of wine and eternal gratitude sufficed.

***

Beating the Spread

With a lifelong fascination of medicine, I finally landed a volunteer job at San Francisco's famed Haight-Ashbury Free Medical Clinic in the mid-seventies, as an intake worker. My father-in-law at the time was a surgeon who I peppered mercilessly with questions every day regarding all things medical, but it was never enough.

Thrilled as I was, I yearned for more than just writing down pertinent data and getting next of kin information. I begged and cajoled for any position that would give me real hands-on experience.

I asked to be trained to give shots, to work in the lab and draw blood, to do physical exams.... I said I'd do anything to get to work alongside one of the docs and get a one-on-one education.

At long last my persistence paid off, and I was offered what was possibly the lowliest hands-on job there was;

"If you sincerely want to work here with the docs... there's a gay men's anal wart clinic held on Saturday mornings. We could use a cheek spreader."

"Ha! That's funny. You had me for a minute though. You're... not... joking?"

"Nope."

I'll tell you what though, there's no better way to prove your worth than to cheerfully accept the worst job in the world. There's also no way better to mobilize your inner creative visualization abilities.

"Oh, that's not liquid nitrogen being poured onto condylomata, it's a mountain mist filtering through the dense canopy of the forest below."

And my gambit to 'beat the spread' eventually paid off, allowing me to rise in the ranks at the various clinics, including medical, drug and alcohol and the prestigious Rock Medicine division, until sometime later where I faced my own legion of earnest newbies who were pleading with me to be able to do;

"Anything. Anything at all."

"Really? Well there's this Saturday clinic... "

Anybody got a lowlier job than that in their C.V.?

***

Two Great Hornbills

Two great hornbills swoop through the jungle canopy and provide enough of a diversionary tactic for a troop of macaques to stage a snatch and grab from the mango seller. Two boys spin on their heels, pull their archer's arms back and fire their slingshot payloads. The monkeys screech with joy as they make a clean escape back to the trees with their bounty.

Our now mangoless lunch continues with the company of two journalists from Quebec, a trio of New Caledonian marine biologists, a Japanese architect and an Irish lass named Mave.

I suppose that's how you'd spell it in English, but it's Gaelic ya know. She is heading off on a Bolivian cattle-drive next.

"We've all got a different bucket list don't we now?!".

A troop of Canadian ravers pass by with their own 'bucket list', theirs are filled with cheap rum and pineapple juice.

'Special today: drink 2 bucket, next one free'.

One of the girls tosses a Styrofoam box with the remains of her Pad Thai off a sea wall and into the mangroves below exclaiming;

"It's OK the tide is coming back in soon."

It took great restraint not to unceremoniously send her off the same sea wall after her trash. Too many witnesses I suppose...

It is inconceivable to me that people litter.

But before my mood can devolve too much, a flock of fruit bats pass overhead and make me think of Ringwraiths, a monitor lizard scurries down a trail and a trillion cicadas reaching a fever pitch drown out the rest of my thoughts.

And the surf beckons.

***

Czech point Charlie...

I wore gloves tonight. Northern Thailand and its cold enough to suit up. Go figure. But it got me thinking about frozen memories.

I was visiting a Bavarian girlfriend in the early nineties. She was a quick-witted cardiologist. She had a bawdy laugh and filled out a dirndl the way the manufacturers had intended. She was amazed to learn that I didn't drink beer, as I'd never really cared for the stuff. That was deemed to be almost an affront to her German heritage, so she said;

"OK we drive to Prague. We go to where beer comes from."

It was late December, early January at the latest. It was cold - northern European cold. We were only an hour or two from the Czech border. The traffic, which consisted of a thousand eighteen-wheelers transporting goods across the curtain, which until recently had been iron, were 'railroaded' on the roadsides and in most of the lanes awaiting inspections. Some of these guys sat in line for up to three days waiting to inch up through the ice towards the check point.

Not a big fan of lines myself and, with nothing to declare, we made it swiftly to the border. Just past the stone-faced immigration guards who exhaled a constant steam of cigarette smoke and frozen breath while pretending to look at documents, was an impossibly long chorus line of nearly naked teenaged prostitutes.

Dozens of them wearing sequined hot pants and skimpy red brassieres which were flashed momentarily as each car passed, from underneath short fox or rabbit stoles. These were girls from Romania, Macedonia, Slovenia and many other Eastern European countries that turned a blind eye to human trafficking.

It was startling, saddening, but would make a great photo.

A line of red-brassiere-flashing girls set against a backdrop of grey trucks and white snow. This would be one to show the folks back home.

Continuing our two-lane country road towards Prague, about twenty minutes past the check point, I felt or rather sensed two rapidly approaching cars from behind. They were Ladas, the infamous utilitarian Russian box cars. I turned around to watch their race. Just then one of the cars drove in the opposing lane and overtook us.

The second car stayed where it was, right behind us.

The lead car then swerved right in front of us and screeched to a halt, while the follow car did the same, boxing us in front and back.

The rest became a slow-motion reality play, as two huge trench-coat wearing thugs emerged. They had long slick black hair, dark eyes with darker circles under them.

Their coats had prominent bulges on their sides, and they wore gold chains and gold rings. A lot of them. Thug number one went over to my girlfriend's window on the driver's side. Thug number two came around to my side. I rolled down my window and as innocently as I could, said;

"Hi, can I..."

And then BOOM. That was as far as I got before his extended right ring-wearing fist collided with my face. My lip split and I was now spraying blood onto him which seemed to make him even angrier. He continued his reach into the car, snatched the Minolta from my lap, prodded open the case and fully extended and exposed my roll of 35mm film.

Behind my new friend was a ditch, which then gave way to a field of frozen corn.

There was no decision-making confusion in his face. It was a done deal, and I knew it. This was my time to Czech out. My girlfriend was screaming in German at thug number one with much the same response as I was getting, nothing. She was still unharmed though.

And then like the *deus ex machina* that we all hope for from time to time, an old man drove up from seemingly out of nowhere. He was quite old but still wore his World War 2 uniform proudly. Perhaps he owned no other clothes. He sized the situation up immediately and delivered a stern rebuke the thugs who then slowly and without a word, retreated and drove off.

Just like that they were gone.

Profuse thanks to the veteran for saving our lives, we too drove off. We had no choice but to go in the same direction as the thugs, as there was no option at that point.

We made our first route change as quickly as possible. We drove in silence for a bit until my girlfriend regained her composure and protested with;

"Oh we must go to police!"

I looked at her incredulously, surprised at her naiveté, and said;

"Are ya kidding? Those WERE the police!"

The Czech border being one of the many spots in the world where the political lines aren't the only ones that get blurred.

Anyway I still had a beer to experience, so on to Prague we continued.

***

Dateline: U Fleku beer house

Erected in 1499, it has been continuously brewing beer for five hundred years. They make a thick dark brown beer that is a meal in and of itself.

The place can host up to twelve hundred patrons, with multiple rooms that have groups of lederhosen wearing men clashing steins to the bawdy sounds of the house oom pah pah band, as well as a main bar which is also from central casting. Multiple steins are slid down the mahogany bar like pucks in a shuffleboard game, each deftly aimed towards the waiting fingers of the customers. It was delicious.

Returning to the States sometime later, I proudly announced to my friends that I was no longer a beer virgin and that I liked the stuff now. My good friend at the time said;

"Well, welcome aboard", and thrust a can of Coors into my hand.

I sadly counted the days until I could return to Prague.

***

Ichigo Ichi-eh

One of the guiding bits of wisdom that I've tried to incorporate into my life, is the Japanese sentiment; *Ichigo Ichi-e*. It essentially means that you may have only this one meeting, this one encounter, so make it as full and complete as you can. It is an especially helpful maxim for a wanderer.

On my first big foray into the wild, I had the great fortune to be seated next to a stunning blonde woman, who it turns out was a university student in the US but was heading home to Japan for the holidays.

I told her of my open-ended travel plans in Asia, and that at some point they would also include Japan.

She was French but had grown up essentially Japanese. Before deplaning in Tokyo, she scribbled down her parents address on a scrap of paper and said that if I ever found myself in Kobe, that I should look them up.

About a year later I did just that. It was an age and time before the Internet or cell phones, so I just showed up. I wasn't hoping for anything save for a childish thought of an expectant note that had been laying in a drawer by the door, addressed 'to the guy I fell in love with on the flight last year'. It was not to be, but I was welcomed with open arms anyway by her mother.

I was a random guy with a backpack in the early eighties on a suburban doorstep in Kobe, Japan. She led me straight away to a private semi-attached six tatami guest house, with sliding shoji doors that separated the main home. She told me I was welcome to stay as long as I liked. It was an extraordinary gesture, which I accepted for three days.

In the evening I met the patriarch, my seat-mate's father, who was a French industrialist who had relocated to Japan in the fifties. After our first meal, he brought me to a room that I recall being vacuum sealed.

There was a tight-fitting door that opened with a whoosh, and inside I was astonished to see a collection that would not have been out of place in an Indiana Jones movie. The walls were covered with ancient calligraphic scrolls and intricately carved Katana samurai swords.

I remember asking him if he could read the scrolls to which he gave the most unusual answer. He said;

"*Mais bien sur*. You do not have a woman just to show her. You must comprehend."

He then grabbed a bottle of pear brandy and brought me into his study where we talked about art, politics and the world.

The morning I left, my seat-mate's dad gave me some gifts to secrete away into my backpack under the promise of never selling them or giving them away, as he'd selected them just for me.

Who does this kind of thing?

He gave me a lacquerware bowl to always keep me fed and a figurine that he said was over a hundred years old, named Kitano Tenmangū which he'd chosen especially for me. He wrapped the gifts in a piece of ancient red silk and presented them in a formal manner, the way one does to a friend you know you will not see again.

I treasure them to this day.

And in the random beauty of the Internet age, on a sleepless night recently I did a search for my seatmate from thirty-five years ago. I stumbled upon a woman with a hyphenated married name that included the surname I had remembered. It gave her birthplace as... Kobe.

It is so rare to get a decent closure in life, and I'd always wanted to express my gratitude and appreciation for all their kindnesses, and most of all to show that their gifted treasures had remained safe and sound. She wrote me back almost immediately, expressing astonishment and pleasure at my having reached out with good memories.

Her father is still alive and would be receiving my update shortly.

"Kitano Tenmangū is popular with students praying for success in exams because the deity was in his life a man of literature and knowledge."

***

Russian Market

Speaking the little bit of Behasa Malay I've managed to retain with the adorably flirtatious Muslim Roti girls, I just couldn't help but feel a touch of sadness for the broad brush of fear and judgement they get swept up into by the headline readers.

But then again, I spend half my life apologizing as well.

Years ago I met a woman at the infamous Russian Market in Phnom Penh. We had both been reaching for the same Louis Armstrong album; Jazz - the true lingua franca. There was a distinct air of wariness about her, which naturally I had to engage.

Turns out she was an attaché with the Indonesian embassy.

We inevitability chatted about the state of the world and current politics. She confessed that she'd never met an American like me, and said that;

"Oh, if there were only ten percent of westerners that thought like you, we'd all have a chance."

I reassured her with higher numbers than that.

Continuing now with my ambassadorial duties one roti shop at a time.

***

John Fengler

Huarache

I was visiting a pal in Panama. Upon request he took me to a 'lil' ol' shoemaker' who'd been making Huarache sandals for generations, as had his father and his father's father. His shop was no more than a shack with a corrugated tin roof and a pile of tanned and tanning leather. He bid me a good day and said;

"Señor please stand on this paper."

He drew a crude outline of my feet with a magic marker, gave me a gold capped smile and said;

"*Listo mañana*" - ready tomorrow.

I wore those Huarache sandals every day for several years. They were by far the most comfortable footwear I'd ever worn and worth every bit of the $4 I'd spent on them. The straps broke from time to time and got re-stitched. The soles wore out and got replaced, and their shape altered over time to the point of unbearable pain, but I continued to wear them past the point of reason. I felt loyal to the shoemaker and to the good times the shoes had given me. I continued to wear them out of habit. Leaving my bungalow barefoot yesterday, not able to bear the discomfort any longer, I grabbed a pair of flip flops from a tourist market and checked out of the bungalow.

I left those handmade Panamanian sandals on the porch in the hopes they might give a gentler walk, for a while longer, to someone for whom they might be a better fit.

***

The Cartographers

I have a particular memory associated with touring through Mae Hong Son province that I've never shared, as it was profoundly humiliating. But alas, the time has come.

I was in the back of a local conveyance, a glorified pickup truck with opposing bench seats called a *songtaew*.

I was traveling with my good friend Claude in the middle of 1980's rural Thai nowhere when an absolutely stunning 'farm girl' got on.

Claude and I immediately began chatting without any inflection that would have given us away. It was an exchange that detailed every hill and valley that we would have liked to explore on our cartographic voyage across the landscape of our new passenger's body. We were quite colorful and detailed in our fantastical exploration and were so immersed in our map making that we had missed our stop by a considerable distance.

We had a brief panicked discussion on how to get back to where we had intended to go, when the expressionless subject of our objectification politely turned towards us and, in perfect Queen's English, suggested that we ask the driver to turn around after she got off and deliver us back to where we had hoped to go. We were mortified, deeply impressed and grateful for the assistance. It is to date the smallest I have ever felt. It was an enormous lesson to learn and one that I've carried with me lo these many years: be respectful, never assume, and always stay out of striking distance.

***

R.I.P Leon Russell

In eighth grade English class I sat behind the curviest girl in the whole school, Dana Fiedler. The bell rang one day in 1971, and as she stood up and turned to leave, she caught my eyes completely transfixed on her chest.

She said; "Jesus, John... what?"

I stammered before broadening my gaze to take in the entirety of her t-shirt which had a giant photo of a guy with a name underneath. I hadn't heard of him before but said;

"Oh... I just love Leon Russell so much."

I decided then and there to learn all I could about the man and his music, and inadvertently became a huge fan. But still forty-five years on I absolutely cannot hear mention of his name without conjuring up that t-shirt.

***

Midnight Express

In the late seventies I had the curious fortune to befriend a guy whose story had terrorized a generation; my generation.

His name was Billy Hayes. He had authored an account of his harrowing days inside a Turkish prison and titled it; *Midnight Express*. The book was subsequently made into a Hollywood film which had one of its premieres in San Francisco that I attended with him. I asked Billy afterwards if he could reconcile some of the differing accounts between the disturbing book and the terrifying movie.

He gave me one of the most straightforward answers ever. He paused, then picked up with;

"I'll tell you honestly, I had some significant debts, financial and ethical that I needed to repay to family and others, and if that meant compromising the story a bit for the film makers, well then so be it."

It is common folklore that the notorious prison where he stayed in Istanbul is now a Four Seasons hotel. While not exactly true, it's true enough, and represents yet another fascinating historical transformation following in the vein of Mamula Fort in Montenegro, which had been one of Mussolini's concentration camps and is now a luxury spa.

Today I found myself looking for ghosts while touring the old Chiang Mai Women's Correctional Institution.

Historically a surprisingly progressive prison which taught crafts and trades that had practical application upon the women's release. It too is now a relic in the middle of a city with a high property value. It is being demolished and will be replaced with yet another high-end resort. And the re-birth cycle continues.

***

Dispatch from Soi Cowboy

I brought my Thai girlfriend down from the Great North to Bangkok for a weekend on the town. We dined at Hemingway`s and wined at Above 11. We listened to jazz at Whisgar's and got shouted at by Bautista over the loudspeakers in Havana Social. We even went for a Turkish coffee and saw Muslims on Soi 3.

Up Sukhumvit we strolled, skirting masseurs in skirts and dodging the dodgy. Past the 'new' porno stands, the 'old' Thai relic stands, nunchucks, Bin Laden lighters, crickets, coconuts and Cialis stalls.

Honeymooning men leering over street side sports bar counters winced as their newlywed wives dug fingers of contempt into their thighs.

"Hey, it's all part of the 'all inclusive' trip, Honey."

The heady mix of fish with garlic and a waft of sewer almost overpowered the smell of a hundred camphor tubes being snorted at any given time. And, of course, the ubiquitous shepherds of the flock, the soi dogs kept a laconically watchful eye on everything from their gutter view perches on the air-conditioned steps of 7-Eleven.

"Well, where would you like to go next, dear?" I ask.

"You know, I never see sexy dancing show before. Maybe can go?"

"Ha-ha, that's funny. No, really, where do you want to go?"

"No, I serious, want to see; if you OK with that?" she asks.

"Oh. Um. Hhmm. Well, I'll ask the concierge at that hotel over there if he knows where we might find one…"

"You don't know from before? I think maybe you know."

"Hhmm."

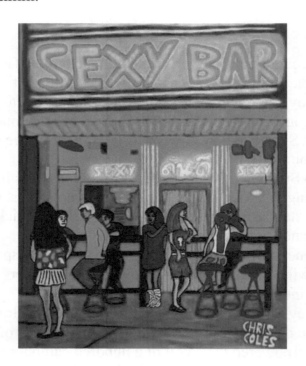

Walking down 'Cowboy', alternately getting grabbed and ignored depending on the level of perception of the hot-pant clad barkers – some seeing I was 'in tow', others not caring and some respecting the invisible 'off the market' sign that a couple heralds.

I turned to her and said,

"OK, here's the deal. You have to promise not to judge this, and whatever you do, you have to promise not to judge me for this. Your idea, your country, your *soi* and it was all here before the both of us."

My real hesitancy was of course being recognized and perhaps warmly greeted by staff members who may have me confused with a real Cowboy punter from another time.

Into Long Gun we went.

We plopped into one of the thigh high booth benches and sunk into the show. The benches filled with tourists holding bootlegged copies of *The Hangover Part II*, a handful of nervously smiling bachelorettes, some grizzled expats and corporate expense account guys sporting dayglow white Oxford shirts that were bathed in black light, their grins responding to the girls who were bathing each other in cheap detergent astride kiddie pools on stage.

Four girls in thigh high black boots, wearing thongs and holding bullwhips queued up just off stage, and thirty pre-poured 'lady drinks' lined up on the bar waiting in abeyance – a stench of urine and lime roiling out from behind the beaded curtain.

"Honey, what about those girls with whips? Are they sadist?"

"Beats me."

My eyes were focused on my girlfriend's reactions. Her eyes were fixed upon gyrating pelvis on the dais. I looked at her expectantly. She enthusiastically said;

"They all so different. Really, I think *pooying* all the same down there. So interesting. Which one you like?"

She sat with her elbows on the counter, her hands propping up her chin. I began to relax. A couple of *sangsom* sodas later the *mamasan* came over to us and took hold of my girlfriend's hand. She said,

"You know, 90 percent of the women who come in here, *farang* or Thai, look either angry or they only half-look out of embarrassment. You are looking fascinated. You are not shy at all, and you are very pretty."

The *mamasan* then shot me a cautious glance, and in Thai asked her if she wanted a job. My girlfriend smiled broadly and said,

"Oh, thank you so much. No!"

I asked her if she really was OK with this whole scene. She said,

"Is normal, you know. Many beautiful girl in the world and normal for guys to look. I have no problem with you looking only. I'm prettier than them anyway. Up to you."

Spat out through the grimy half curtains of the club into the maelstrom of doe-eyed girls fawning over the hunters and punters, the soul savers and lost souls, the *mamasan* followed us out, gave us an enigmatic smile then turned towards the *somtam* stand as we head once again towards the hall of smoke and mirrors that is the Sukhumvit road.

***

The chateau

Long before the advent of low-cost airlines that would cut the thirteen-hour trip from Bangkok to Chiang Mai down to fifty minutes, there was the overnight train which was the preferred mode of transport.

Third class was unthinkable for a long ride to a westerner of any means, and first class was isolating and out of reach cost wise for anyone with a backpack and a travel budget. That left second class which was further divided into 'fan' cars and air-con cars.

The fan cars were the epitome of idealized Southeast Asian romanticism, with toggle lever windows and teak slat covers that would invariably stay open all night filling the car with the rattle of steel wheels and torpid Asian air. But the car would soon fill with diesel trailing from the engine and the smell of soot would be all consuming. The air-con cars would've been able to keep frozen meat from ever thawing and no one travelled with winter wear anyway, so the fan car it was.

On this trip I had the lower berth. Opposite me was a French couple and their young boy. We struck up conversation, drank local beer and chatted mostly in French for a good part of the night. I pretended they understood me, and they never let on otherwise.

Arriving at dawn we traded contact information with halfhearted; 'yes if you're ever in America…' and 'yes if you ever in France…' And wished each other *bon sejours*.

A couple of months later while safely ensconced in my California mountain home the phone rang.

"Allo, Jean? We meet in the train in Thailand. You say we can stay in your house?!"

"Oh yeah, wow nice to hear from you. When will you be in America?"

"Ah we arrive your home in four hour."

And so they did; Mom, Dad, kid, luggage and toys for a week. To their credit they brought a feast with them as well. All was good until Claire asked where my fondue pot was? I said;

"Um it's in the department store waiting for me to buy it."

"OK never mind, we make do."

I did have an electric wok which she ingeniously lined with aluminum foil, and *voila*. It was a very nice week of country French living with my humble backpacker family.

Two years later it was time for payback as I found myself at Lyon train station.

"Hello, Claire? You stayed in my house in California..."

"Yes sure, Michel will pick you up *tout suite*."

A late model Saab whooshed to a halt about nine minutes later and a tan, robust and tailored Michel jumped out of the car to kiss me on both cheeks. He said;

"OK we have to go quick, or we'll be late."

"Late for what?"

"Oh some friend of mine have a party in the countryside."

"Oh ya know I only have my travel jeans and this t-shirt..."

"Don't worry, zese are good friend."

And then like the Millennium Falcon he drove at a nauseating speed around the whiplash inducing curves of the Beaujolais hills until pulling up forty-five minutes later at a chateau. It was a Bond villain's type building, with convertible sport cars and Rolls Royce's being guided to gravel parking slots around the giant central fountain by an endless line of uniformed valets.

There were a lot of plunging necklines decorated with pearls and tan, handsome men wearing provocatively unbuttoned pressed white shirts and polished black shoes. I could not have felt more out of place.

Inside the chateau it was immediately clear that it had been converted into a vintner's paradise with hundreds of wine barrels stacked inside the cool, dank building *ancienne*.

There was a fifteen-foot banquet table that had apples sticking out of roast pig's mouths, piles of meats, wheels of cheese, strawberries, grapes, figs and pate. There were four men wearing medallion adorned sashes atop some sort of conquistador uniforms standing at attention behind it.

My friend guided me to a reception line and whispered that this was the grand presentation of the Beaujolais Nouveau and I would meet his friend who was the mayor of the region. There were probably thirty people queued up to congratulate the vintners and their royal sponsors. I shook several hands without sensing even the slightest bit of mockery at my attire.

When it was my turn to meet the mayor, my friend gave me a warm introduction as "*mon ami Americaine. Nous nous sommes recontres en Thailande.*" The mayor dutifully shook my hand and asked if I could speak French? I said;

"A bit, but I drink wine, the language of the world."

What can I tell ya? It just came out. He froze, turned fully towards me with a semi-teared up eye, put his arm around my shoulders and walked us both from the reception line leaving a lot of perplexed faces. He smiled broadly and said;

" I love zis guy!"

I guess it was the right thing to say. He toured me around the rows of barrels and then gave me an Inservice on the new releases. We walked over to one barrel; he leaned in conspiratorially saying;

"Don't waste your time wis zis one, is shit."

He then deposited me with a wink at the good wine and wished me well. Moments later the four sashed men pulled medieval trumpets from a table below them and heralded an invocation of the spirits for the new wine. Speeches were made, toasts were given, cheeks were kissed.

Back on the road after a long day and an unexpectedly longer evening we arrived at the not so humble abode of my French backpacker family. Arched stone doorways that led to thick-beamed hallways, a Citizen Kane sized fireplace and original issue Roman stone garden walls.

My friend was surprised at how nonplussed I was regarding the lavish style he lived in. He had been as humble and at ease in 'zecond class' as he was here in Xanadu. He was a model of humility. He said;

"You know my family is here now six generation. We are Lyon. If you want to buy some souvenir it is up to you, but zat will be your only expense while you are here with us."

The following days were filled with tours of Interpol, fish markets and Klaus Barbie's last known residence. Meals were at restaurants that seemed always to have the best table waiting and respectful bonhomie from the staff. We ate salted bone marrow, plates of braised pork that were served inside hollowed out pig hooves, creamed fish, red wine sausage, too much cheese and many other gout inducing dishes 'Lyonnaise'.

My sendoff was in *'une caverne'*.

"For sure you are ze first tourist to ever come here."

It would be fun to think so. An ancient subterranean wine cellar turned into a wonderfully claustrophobic jazz club with brilliant acoustics thanks to the low, curved and unventilated stucco ceilings. We made one final stop for a personal indulgence in a Franciscan monastery that was famed for its preserves. I secreted a couple of jars of raspberry into my backpack only to have the confiture confiscated by French customs officials at Charles de Gaulle airport.

"I am sorry Monsieur, is because of your country's liquid policy." I smirked and replied;

"Ah George W. Bush preventing the spread of jam, is he?"

I told him to tell his wife that they were gifts from *'mon ami Americaine'*. He told me that unfortunately they would go in the trash.

"So much more the shame."

"Comment?"

"*C'est triste.*"

***

Chez Julien

Whenever I pass by Chez Julien, I'm reminded of a time I went there for lunch with one of my wives.... some years ago. There was only one other table of diners, so I approached them, showed my camera, gestured towards my wife and said;
"Would you mind... a photo?"
A woman at the table let out an exasperated sigh, threw her hair back and affected a pose, saying;
"Well OK."
Confused for a moment I said;
'No, I was asking if you would mind taking our photo?'
Another woman at the table then stood up brusquely and said;
"Monsieur, do you not know who zis woman is?"
I admitted that surely, I did not.
"Well she is ze most famous diva in all of Paris."
'Ya don't say?! Do you think she could take our photo?'
To the diva's credit, she broke pose, threw her head back in laughter, looked at us and said;
"It would be a pleasure, Monsieur."

***

Holly

About 30 years ago I was in one of life's doldrums. My best friend at the time dragged me out to a party in Silicon Valley, saying;
"Come on, it'll be good for you. Maybe you'll meet someone?!"
I declined at first; saying I had nothing to say to a bunch of engineers. He told me that if anyone asked me what I did, to just say that I was an IBM chair. I didn't know what that meant but went with it.

He neglected to tell me his company was in the middle of a hostile takeover. He loved a good practical joke. Sure enough I found myself in a group at the party and spewed out my rehearsed line, in the hopes it would quell any further inquiries.

No sooner did the 'IBM chair' words leave my mouth, than a stunning blonde spun around, lock eyes with me and say;

"Well FUCK you!!"

My friend couldn't have been more pleased with himself.

I spent the next five years with that woman. Three of them were phenomenal. Two of them less so. We remained lovingly acrimonious ever since. Much to my relief she became someone else's burden some years after we split up, and we were able to remain good friends.

Before we separated, she took a trip to Europe and brought me back a Swiss Army knife that I use to this day. One uneventful evening, I was opening a bottle of wine with it and thought to take a photo of it and post it on her Facebook, to let her know she was still in my thoughts.

I was stunned to be greeted by a page of remembrance and a host of 'rest in peace' posts from family and friends. She would have been about 50.

I was all set to get in another pissing match with her tonight, something we did well and enjoyed. She was a great sparring partner and, in our time, a great friend, lover, and ally.

Well you won this round kiddo but watch out!!

***

TripAdvisor

The course, crushed rock-laced razor-wire that passes for sand here, is slick with rancid kitchen oil, which is thankfully only visible in the few spots that aren't trampled down by the indolent hordes of loud, corpulent Euro-trash who line the beach alongside broken beer bottles and used condoms. The water is a mélange of raw sewage and deformed dead fish. The mythical pink dolphins, nothing more than Cthulhu-faced sea vermin.

The resort itself is an entomologist's dream, the mattresses an undulating mass of lice and bed bugs.

The 'cuisine' which was clearly inspired by the chefs from the Devil's Island prison, features inedible lumps of mashed weevils and heron droppings. The owners are boorish, oppugnant misanthropes, better suited to Stasi basement listening cells.

Don't come here. Tell everyone you know not to come to Le Petit Saint Tropez on Khanom beach, in Nakhon Si Thammarat, Thailand.

It's a horrible, terrible, no-good place. Believe me!

***

John Fengler

Dateline: Lonely Planet days.

The real ones where entries included tips on traveling. Real tips; how to skirt this or that border, which crossing had more visa friendly officers, where the 'off the beaten path' truly was. Another time.

I was armed with the first edition LP Thailand, which was about 3/4 of an inch thick for the whole country. I followed a lead to an island in the Gulf which was about a hundred kilometers south of the capitol. It was called Ko Si Chang. There was a rumor of a partially built Royal palace that had been abandoned in the late nineteenth century when the French had short-lived dreams of occupation. I didn't need much provocation for an adventure.

There was no regular transport to the island that I was aware of, but I managed to finagle a ride on a fishing boat. The boat driver gave me a bit of a concerned look and said;

"But nothing there for you", meaning no hotels, restaurants etc.

I said that he just sealed the deal. I had my backpack. I managed to get a local motorcyclist to take me into the jungle to the site of the old palace. I also let him know it was OK to leave me there. Crazy falang.

Truly a remarkable sight, an incomplete royal residence that was now, one hundred years later, being ingested by the surrounding jungle. The marble floor of the grand entryway, where I eventually spent the night, columned balustrades lining a swimming pool that had never been filled with anything but rainwater; and mysterious stairways that led to nowhere, or maybe some Hobbit world only accessible by wearing a certain ring.

I awoke rested and unmolested by anything larger than a mosquito. Filled with wonder I set out on foot for the coast. It was an island after all, how lost could I get?

I was crossing a bit of arid midlands when I came upon a rock face. It looked to be an easy climb, and far more promising than the long slog around it. I hefted up the rock and was about twenty feet up when I threw my hand over the top. Ready to hoist up and over, I saw and then felt a thousand fire ants racing down my hand and arm. They live in boxes made of leaves which are held together by their spit. They are virtually undetectable to the untrained eye, especially a blind one lifting over a ledge. They bite and it hurts. I had to fight my instinct to pull my hand back in retreat, as I would have plummeted to certain injury if not more. Mind over matter works until the adrenaline wears off, so over the top I went. Brushing them off and gathering my wits I headed off again, this time on a slightly more elevated but no less arid plain. But now I could see the Gulf.

About twenty minutes further I turned and noticed a saffron robed monk standing in the openness. He had appeared out of nowhere. He smiled at me and then disappeared into the ground. I am prone to hyperbole, but not to illusion.

I ran to where I had just seen him and found a hole in the ground. Peering into it my new monk friend was suspended in the darkness and holding onto a vine.

He smiled again and gestured me to follow him. Of course I did. It was a cave entrance. The cool dank moist air was a relief from the dry arid air I had been breathing. There were recessed Buddha images carved into the limestone and Buddhist adornments all around.

I followed him in amazement until reaching a cathedral, as they are called in the spelunking world; an expansive high-ceilinged part of a cave. I looked up with my mouth agape in wonder. The monk slid to my side and gently reached up to my chin and closed my mouth. He smiled and pointed at the roof of the cave and mimicked the flapping motion of bats. He gave me the international symbol of 'he who looks at cave roof with mouth open, eats bat guano'.

Continuing my tour of this subterranean temple, we wound up at a horizontal opening with an expansive view of the Gulf. Entered by descending into a field and exited onto a sea front vista. There were many monks there laughing at unknown things and completely unsurprised by my presence. One was peeling hard boiled eggs and tossing them to what I took to be their pet monitor lizard.

I didn't know one could domesticate them but hell they were monks. Just some more magic I supposed. Like an idiot I went over to pet it. THWACK went its prehensile tail to my inner thigh, about 2 inches from Vienna boys choir destination. I had a welt for years from that. Somehow that endeared me to no end with my new hosts. We sat there without a word in common for a while. And then with no discernable signal, save maybe some high pitched 'monk whistle', they all stood up and then gestured that I should enter a previously unseen chamber in the cave.

There was a wooden platform raised about a foot off the ground. I was instructed to take my flip flops off and sit on the platform. I sat there with a goofy smile for a few minutes when the grand poobah came in. He was straight out of central casting where they call for a wizened seer.

I wanted to rub his belly. He sat across from me; a little bit higher on a second platform. He crossed his legs, assessed me for a moment, and then in decent English said;

"What do you want to know?"

Really? REALLY?

I was in my early twenties, a post Sartre infused graduate and a traveler. I wanted to know everything. Why are we here? What is the difference between sin and crime? Is there life after death?

My mind raced. I knew I had stumbled onto a great, seminal moment in my life. No time to question the whys of it. Boots on the ground.

I wanted to ask something accessible, linguistically as well as philosophically.

I didn't want to squander this opportunity but didn't want to come off as an idiot either. I said;
"I want to know how to meditate".
That's the best I could come up with. He beamed back at me. It was the right question.
He then scooted a bit closer to me and reached over to adjust my posture. He then lowered his eyelids partially, into the Sukhothai pose, and slowly, beautifully, rhythmically inhaled, all the while drawing out the sound 'Booooooooo', and then at the apogee of his breath he exhaled and chanted; 'Daaaaaaaaaaaaa.' It was a seamless breath, much as the circular breathers of the didgeridoo have mastered.
I practiced in front of him for a bit until he gave me a 'too late for you grasshopper' look and released me to my previous hosts. I ate rice with the monks for a day, taught them a few words in English and fended off their great attempts to tattoo me. It was a monastic hermitage I found out. It was a particular destination for true disciples from temples all over the country and I had found it by accident, or providence.

The next day I took my leave and headed over to the other side of the island, much the same route I had taken to get where I was.
I walked for several hours across the same arid expanse as before. I then caught sight of the farthest shore right before the walls of the path obscured the coast with a sharp descent. I followed a now curiously well-worn trail, came around a final blind corner and encountered the next most extraordinary vision. On either side of the trail, which had suddenly turned tropical, were two lovely Thai sirens wearing long traditional silk wraps. Each was holding two halves of a freshly cut pomegranate. They gave me warm smiles that betrayed no surprise at my presence. Quite the contrary, as it seemed they had been expecting me.

They both then turned and ushered me to a teak home which jutted out over the water, with its Gulf end supported by wooden piers. There were buckets of crabs, fishing nets, a steaming pot of soup suspended over a charcoal fire and a couple of teak fishing boats. They sat me down in what I suspected was the living room. It was the closest comparison I could make being that the whole place was more or less open air.

I waited for the next surprise. A short while later a man came over and sat across from me. He was about ten years older than me and had a gentle but concerned look about him. He had things on his mind. I was his guest as is the Thai way but an uninvited one. I looked him in the eyes, pointed at myself and said;
'Johhhhnnnn', and then smiled.
He paused, gave a sardonic smile and said;
"Name's Paul. I used to be V.P. of BBD&O advertising in L.A."
What??? How? What? Why? And who were those girls?
"It's a small island. We knew you were here three days ago. Expected you to turn up sooner but guess you found the monks. I'm Thai by birth and this was the family homestead."
His tone became forlorn, continuing with;
"Dad was a crab fisherman and I inherited the place, so I'm stuck here."
"Stuck?" I exclaimed. "People would kill to be stuck here!"
He gave a deflated smirk and said;
"Yeah, you want to buy it?"
"Um well no but..."
"Yeah, nobody else does either. It's a golden albatross. Anyway let's eat some crab and you can tell me about the world. I'll have one of the girls ferry you back to shore later. It's the only way out of here unless you want to hike across the tundra again."

We talked until the sun began to set. He said he had to tend to his traps. I thanked him for his hospitality and wished him good luck. One of the sirens had changed into Thai fisherman's pants and a Chinese shirt.

She smiled that enigmatic Thai smile and silently steered me back to the world.

***

Only floss the ones you want to keep

It wasn't compassion fatigue as much as a sympathetic indifference. You get to a point when you've just seen it all. You haven't stopped caring as much as just lost sensation. It's nerve damage.

I had my epiphany at 3d and Evans, at 3 a.m. in the aptly named Hunter's Point section of San Francisco. It was in the middle of a four-lane road, at the double yellow lines.

A bustling avenue of commerce to the shipyards by day, a ghost town of absentee landlord gangsters by night.

There was a *War of the Worlds* streetlight glaring down on us and not a soul in sight.

Bisecting the yellow lines was the lifeless body of a thirty-year-old black woman. The half of her face that was still intact appeared to have been attractive in life, which in my estimation had been about twenty minutes earlier.

We are steeped in protocol, procedure and rote medicine, much as any Marine worth his salt can strip down and reassemble his side arm in his sleep.

We mercilessly adhere to these standards and at some advanced point in our careers, teach them. But the years also let you learn to recognize plain old dead, without having to go in for the unnecessary and oft-times disruptive bells and whistles of intervention.

The well-meaning folks that arrive shortly before us on these sorts of calls, as is the nature of pre-hospital care, were not always as well attuned. On this occasion one of them decided to attempt revival. As I surveyed and hoped to preserve this crime scene, one of the guys had unceremoniously reached over and grabbed a large rock that was near our victim's head on the double yellow line. It was a bloodied rock which he had gently placed under our victim's neck, hoping to open her airway so he could initiate CPR.

I caught my partner's gaze as we squinted in disbelief. We both deflated in exasperation and silently chose not to break the blue line with admonishment about using murder weapons as rescue tools, thereby relinquishing any hope of salvage or preservation.

The blue line is the one that protects you on the next call when you need police crowd control. The line that swears in deposition that our 'metal restraints' (some call them handcuffs), were warranted on the combative patient and not excessive.

And it's the line that doesn't give you a ticket as you're blazing up the freeway at ninety-five miles an hour at the end of your shift at 5 a.m., when you're hoping to see your suburban bedroom before the light breaks. Breaking light will fuck up any chance you had of having anything close to resembling a normal night's sleep.

As well it was already after 3 a.m., which denotes the ebb tide of motivation.

Evidence as well as integrity of the scene was already shot to hell, and well, she wasn't gonna get any more dead, so we figured 'he' might be able to look his rebellious teenager in the eye tomorrow, or his slighted wife, or the boys down at the Slovenian hall and have a sobering tale of heroism to tell. After allowing him his face-saving moments of attempted glory, I put my 'comrade in arms' hand on his shoulder, shook my head solemnly and stated the time of death;

"Zero-three-seventeen. Thanks for your help, gentlemen."

The chain of command as well as the legal rights of succession dictate that the body may be relinquished to our custody, thereby releasing all other attending agencies to some slumber, or another call. It also remands us to corpse watch until the coroner arrives, which at that hour of the day has him pushing his suburban beeper under his pillow until his sleeping wife shoves his shoulder in consternation. He also knows damn well that we're a captive audience and that dammit he's gonna grab a cup of instant coffee to drink for the thirty-minute drive to Baghdad by the Bay, and then across the great divide to 'the hood'.

There's a time then, between the catch and release of police and fire agencies, news crews, bystanders, and paperwork, when you are alone in the quiet of the late-night shift with only a dead thirty-year-old woman by your side.

The good thing is you couldn't be dispatched to another call, and you knew how to drag this out to the end of your shift so you could relax after seventeen other calls that day.

And then you find a pack of dental floss in your pocket that along with a free toothbrush were the consolation prizes for your annual checkup and cleaning the day before. You were advised to "floss only the ones you want to keep". It was a sobering warning, so you pull out a foot of string and heed his advice.

You look at the fog line and know the drive over the bridge will be slow as visibility is decreased. You glide over your second molar going for the tricky rim shot of the third, which by all accounts you are lucky to have. You note the irony that you're still wearing latex gloves from the call, much as the dentist himself wore on your visit.

And then a speck of arugula from the sandwich you gulped down three hours ago, with lights and sirens blaring on the way to, 'huh, what was that call?', flies out of your mouth and you trace its trajectory following it down to the ground. And next to it lies the crushed head of a thirty-year-old black woman.

And then you have your epiphany; that you are flossing over a murder victim in the middle of the night and that you are completely unperturbed by this. But you are aware enough to be perturbed by the fact that you are not perturbed. And then you reassess your life, wondering how some over-educated Manhattanite wound up in a uniform standing alone over a corpse in the middle of a four-lane road in the most violent part of an adopted city?
 A part of the city that would not be survivable to you off-duty in blue jeans and a golf shirt, and how utterly invulnerable you feel and are because of it. Because you are one of the good guys, like when you went to the Hell's Angel's den for the stabbing the previous morning, and they tried their best to intimidate you, but you just stared them down saying;
 "Hey, you guys called me!"
 And then it was;
 "Yeah, sorry man, what do you need?"
 And you reassess your compassion, your interest levels and your mortgage. And then you decide something's got to change. But not today. Eventually a white van arrives, and two haggard men step out.
 You both jut your chins in greeting to each other as you silently hand over your paperwork and documentation.
 The coroner sizes up the scene and notes the bloodied rock that had been un-naturally placed under the woman's neck. He raises his eyebrow. You shrug and motion your head over towards the police station. He gives you a wry smile of 'yeah, the usual', thereby silently concluding our responsibilities for this call.

I stroll back to the ambulance and catch the first belt of pre-fog chill as I step in, jarring my partner awake who is the driver this shift. We also don't need to speak. He looks at me, then at his watch. He knows we still have forty-five minutes to kill. We both know it's off to the donut shop with some 'engine trouble'. Try as we might to not be cliche, it's 4:15 a.m. in San Francisco and not a shred of arugula in sight.

***

Just plane wrong

I went for a family reunion in Charleston, South Carolina one summer. Took the red eye from San Francisco landing at the crack of dawn. Feeling my best. I went straight to the car rental counter only to be informed that there was no such reservation under my name in the system.

I would have none of it. I went into full-on indignant New York sales counter rage as is my birthright. I said;

'Listen here, I've been up all night and am in no mood. I know for a fact that I made a reservation for a car on this day and at this time in Charleston, South Carolina!'

This gal gave me a pitying shake of the head and said;

"That may very well be, sir, but this here is Charlotte, North Carolina."

There's a term that Rick Reynolds uses, 'dickhead momentum'.

It's a point in an argument where you realize, in this instance with blinding clarity, that you're wrong, but you just can't stop yourself, continuing with; 'and another thing... '

I did my very best to finesse the crushing realization of my error of not only having booked a car in the wrong city but of having flown into the wrong state. Hands on my hips I lamely countered with;

"Well what am I supposed to do now?"

She good naturedly suggested;

"Why don't you take our free shuttle bus to the Waffle House darlin' and sort yourself out?!"

Accepting defeat I asked how much a rental car was from where we were? She gave me a price and asked for a major credit card. I didn't have one.

"Well how'd you book a car in the first place?"

I told her I used a debit card.

"Well that just ain't gonna work here I'm sorry to say."

'Really?? How 'bout I BUY a car? Can I do that?!'

"Darlin' go get you some waffles and some coffee and then get a taxi to the bus station. That's what I would do."

And so off to the Waffle House I went. Six months ago I went for my one o'clock flight from Sri Lanka back to Thailand. I'd splurged on a business class ticket and arrived 'early' to linger in their lounge, only to be informed that;

"Your ticket was booked for a one a.m. flight, sir."

Shit!

'Well any ideas what to do for twelve hours around here?'

"Sir, that was for one in the morning LAST night!"

'" Soooo..."

"Yes, you'll have to buy a completely new ticket for tonight's flight, and I'm sorry to inform you of a slight fare increase."

"How slight?"

"It's not that long of a flight, sir. Perhaps you should consider coach."

Twelve hours to kill before my new coach flight, I jumped in a taxi and asked the driver to take me to the closest beach resort to the airport. Sri Lanka being an island I figured it couldn't be too far and thought that I'd just plan on lingering interminably by their pool. Twenty minutes under the broiling mid-day sun I went to reception and asked for a day rate on a room. It was of course exorbitant.

I threw myself at the mercy of the court explaining my predicament and asked if they had some shitty little maid's room with no view and no mint on the pillow. I promised not to disturb anything and to be out early enough that they could re-rent the room if need be.

There's some connectivity to people who can view you as an equal, or at least someone who's in a situation they can identify with and can respond to with a level of vulnerability to which they feel comfortable. When you appeal in good spirit, I find that folks generally want to help. It's the universality of good nature.

This woman made a sidelong glance that spoke of; 'well we're not supposed to do this but' and said;

"Well there is a very late check-in tonight, and if you promise to be out by... you can slip me twenty dollars."

A done deal!

I first wrote this in the lobby of a hotel in Bangkok that I booked for the following week. The problem being that I had intended to reserve it for the previous night.

"Yes, sure you can cancel and change your reservation, sir. Of course there will be a one night's cancellation fee."

'But I only booked for one night... riiight.'

I read an interview once with some super model. She said guys always say;

"Where does someone like me get to meet a woman like you?"

She replied;

"Well if you work at Applebee's, you're more likely than not to meet people that go to Applebee's (and have Applebee's anecdotes). Hang out where models do, and you have a better chance of meeting a model. Oh and learn to play the guitar."

Travel a lot and you're bound to have travel mishap anecdotes.

I was hitchhiking across Japan a million years ago. It was only difficult in that no one knew what I was doing as that was a relatively unknown activity there.

Most folks figured a westerner's out-stretched thumb was just another foreign way of saying hello. I got a lot of smiling waves, but it took a while to get a ride.

It was during that time when I began to develop my Zen approach to travel. I had a vague idea of where I wanted to go but realized that wherever I wound up, was where I wanted to be - to a point. It was all part of the trip, warts and all.

And the beat goes on.

***

Nice knockers

Went to hit some balls today and…

When I first settled permanently in Chiang Mai, going on twelve years now, I got wind of the Gymkhana Club.

Of course it was recommended to me by an Australian woman who had a thick accent, which resulted in me spending two weeks diligently looking for the 'Jim Connor's' club. I finally found someone who could do an Oz to Yank translation to set me straight.

Hey, if it was good enough for Somerset Maugham to hang out at a hundred years ago.

I went inside the club and found a young woman who worked there and asked when a good time was to run into single tennis players.

She said;

"Oh, are you looking for some knockers?"

"What??"

"If you want some nice knockers, I have available for you."

"What??"

"I mean people to play tennis with you for 200-baht one hour. What you think I mean?"

It's a Thai/British club as it turns out. Knockers are pro tennis folks. Who knew? Finally I did wind up with a trio who were looking for a fourth to play doubles. Was an incredibly polite Englishman and two no-nonsense Thai women. Before accepting I told them that I wasn't very good, in case they were looking for a more serious player. The guy in the most self-deprecating way that the English seem to excel at, said;

"Oh, neither are we, haha. Please join us."

After the first game the two Thai women came over to me, one saying;

"Oh, we think you kidding around, but *jing jing* you not very good. Maybe you more comfortable at Chiang Mai land courts."

Thais are nothing if not direct. The English guy cast his eyes downward and said;

"They're really not bad courts over there…."

"Really? Yer kicking me out?"

"Well, it's not me you understand, but there are only two courts here, and they do tend to get busy. Tata, ole chap."

***

Cafe de la Paix

Last day of one of my honeymoons; Cafe de la Paix, Paris. It was a tony place that I'd saved a few ducats for. Our mostly uneaten squab laid listless and destined for the dustbin. I thought; 'fuck that, I'm taking it for the flight.'

I asked my server in what I took to be passable French for a 'doggie bag'. She threw her nose into the clouds and walked off. I turned to an elderly couple at the next booth and said;

"Excuse me, but did you, by any chance, observe my exchange with the waitress? Was my French OK? I didn't understand her reaction."

They discussed the exchange between them in depth before the woman solemnly announced;

"Yes, your French is very good. It is because you have... oh how to say in English?"

And then she beamed triumphantly, coming up with the right words;

"Yes, is because you have... no class."

"Oh, thank you. Thank you sooooo much."

***

Virgin

"Excuse me, sir, you want virgin?"

"Come again?"

"Many foreigner looking for virgin, but virgin finished for today. I can tell you another area to look if you like?"

"...What?"

"Oh, sorry, I see you look at salad oil. I think that what you looking for."

***

Lolita

I got 'cruised' by a 16-year-old girl. She and her friend, both of whom broke away from their flight delayed Scandinavian families, conferred from a distance, completely imbued with their secret belief of public invisibility. The friend gave a slight push, with what I imagined to be departing advice of; "just walk by him".

She slowed her pace as she approached my table.

I looked up from my wine glass, having already prepared for this interaction, met her gaze and gave a small and confident smile. It wasn't a lecherous smile, but it certainly wasn't paternal. I conveyed I hope, an appreciation of her awkward yet bold awakening. An acknowledgment of what I believe she is trying to come to terms with; that of her physical and emotional powers that are developing as quickly as her school uniform size is.

She turned the shade of a ripe pomegranate, quickened her stride, then giggled into the waiting side of her friend.

I once heard that baby snakes were potentially more lethal than adult ones, as they haven't developed the mechanism to regulate their venom yet. She will learn blush control soon enough. And with that natural evolution, innocence will recede.

Humbert getting hammered.

***

The Tower of Babel

At the best damn bar for blues night. Spied a guy they must've called 'Tiny', who I imagine had spent the last twenty years in a Bulgarian prison, pumping Chevy engines.

He dropped a significant wad of cash on the floor. I caught his eyes and pointed my finger his way. He stood up and became the Incredible Hulk before me, menacingly flexed. I dropped my index finger towards his feet.

He looked down, and with great surprise gathered up his cash. He then came over, gave me a dangerous smile and put me in a not so gentle head lock, rubbed my scalp and said;

"Hokay, we're good."

Reminded me of another close encounter…

Many years ago I gently rear-ended a car in midtown Manhattan.

It was a bump small enough to not require a mechanic but significant enough to warrant getting out and saying hello. The guy jumped out of his car, puffed up his chest, clenched his fists and marched towards me.

Just as he approached and gave me the universal 'fight or flight' glare, I jutted my chin towards the offending distraction who was just rounding the corner. He stopped and turned towards where I had indicated. He lingered his gaze, then checked his bumper.

He looked at me, nodded with great appreciation and deflated, then silently walked back to his car without comment.

***

L'elephant

"Oh, nice to see you again, Mr. John."
"Oh my god, you see a million tourists a year here. How could you possibly remember me?"
"Oh, you have big fight with your wife last year. Everyone remember you."

***

Iris

I penned this remembrance of my mother, four years to the day after she passed away. For Iris on this strange and mournful day.

When I was ten years old, I lamented to my mom about not having a Halloween costume. She shot back immediately with;
"Why dontcha paint yerself red, stick a broom stick up yer ass and go as a jelly apple!".
I was ten! That story of course couldn't be funnier to me now. My mom was a 'New York broad'. They don't make 'em like that anymore. Haven't in a long time. She called people 'Buster', while flicking cigarette butts at their feet. She took no guff.
I called her up once at her end of days and asked;
"Are you happy, mom?"
Without skipping a beat she replied;
"You know me kid. I'm not happy till you're not happy."

There's a quote in *As Good as It Gets*;
Some of us have great stories, pretty stories that take place at lakes with boats and friends and noodle salad. Just no one in this car.
Adding to the mix has been the constant historical revisionism that has occurred at family gatherings. Rick Reynolds penned a line regarding this phenomenon. He said;
"Somehow my Kafka-esque childhood got turned into a Frank Capra movie."

Those friends who were fortunate enough to have met my mom know she was a unique character.

One of the most common reactions I've gotten from people throughout my life has been;

"Wow, I thought you were exaggerating, John!"

My mom was a witty, defiant, opinionated, and deeply irreverent woman. She loved cigarettes, Rush Limbaugh, the Mafia, Miss Marple, a good fight and most of all me. She was also possibly the funniest person I've ever known.

"Yeah, I'll tell ya kiddo, Phyllis Dillah' got her routine from ME!"

Hard to do her justice without the four-part harmony she deserves, as well as the ninety-five dollars an hour therapy sessions I'd have to pay for you all. She sure knew how to press my buttons but then she placed them there didn't she?!

She has passed, and the world will be a little less caustic, a little bit less wry and a whole lot less hilarious.

For better or for worse I am in part a creation of her wit, her anger and her resolve, and I am a better person for it all and when the floodgate of tears finally opens for me, I am confident they will quickly be washed away by the laughter. It's a family trait after all.

Rest in peace Mom.

**

Bond night

A dozen years ago - shaken and stirred at a US embassy 'Bond night' party in Chiang Mai, I saw a stunning gal dressed in a skintight black latex pantsuit. Was hard to tell the guests from the actual security. She was carrying an Uzi.

I sidled up to her and asked her name.

She responded without looking at me;

"My name Natasha."

"Ha, that's great. No, but seriously, what's your name?"

She turned and bored her eyes into me and snapped;

"I already tell you, is Natasha!"

I continued with my tried-and-true Russian - Wow, you speak my language pickup line;

'Vy ochen krasivaya' (You are very beautiful)

"Yes, I hear zis all ze time."

"Riiight. Of course you do. Forgot where I was for a minute. Seeya..."

***

Mein Kampf

Had a Bavarian girlfriend for a while years ago.

We practiced shuttle diplomacy for a year or so between the US and Germany, seeing each other every two months, with her coming to the States and me going to see her. It was ideal... until it wasn't.

I was at her dad's house for Christmas. We'd just finished walking through a winter wonderland of a storybook town square, admiring Christmas trees in homes that were lit with real candles, drinking hot glühwein and eating delicious sausages… until she told me they were horse meat... but I digress.

Back at her parents' home, I was browsing the family bookshelf and stumbled upon a copy of Mein Kampf. I was completely taken aback and suddenly critically aware of where I was. I pulled it off the shelf and waved it at her with a 'wtf' expression on my face. She looked at me and defensively responded with;

"It's not autographed!"

Ah, point well taken.

***

Labor Day

Just went to my local mechanic to get a couple of lights replaced. Seventeen-year-old kid gave me a 'Hhmm I've never worked on a B'mer before, but I'll figure it out' smirk.

He spent twenty minutes trying to figure out how to remove the headlight and saw that a wire had become disconnected, but the light was fine. He reassembled the front and then replaced a burned-out taillight.

He shyly gave me my bill of $3 and, by way of explanation for the exorbitant rate, showed me the burned-out bulb. I said;

"But what about your time on the headlight?"

He gave me a quizzical look and said;

"Nothing broken. Is free."

This is a kid who makes nine bucks a day if he's lucky, no benefits and undoubtedly fishes for his dinner in the nearby river. I doubled his bill to which he gave me an astonished look of appreciation and a big Thai *wai*.

I just love this place sometimes.

***

Koh phayam

Just been stuck in my craw.

Met a couple of fetuses on the boat the other day as we docked on an obscure island I wasn't familiar with. I asked if there was any electricity at all on the island and they both smirked and dismissively snorted;

"Well if you... need that sort of thing."

I looked them straight in their suburban blonde dreadlocks and said;

"Ya know... I was island hopping in these waters decades before your parents even knew which end of the coconut to squeeze to get their suntan oil!!"

OK I didn't say that, but I did warn them about the Burmese '*rasta*' spider that likes to burrow into matted hair though, then hopped off and wished them well on their bio-diesel powered flight back to the States.

Ah kids today. Ain't got no respect.

***

Mentor

With the beauty of the Internet age, and the brilliance of nostalgia, I was randomly tracked down by one of my oldest and closest friends from several lifetimes ago. He was my travel mentor when this all began. We reminisced and updated, and I was reminded of one of the best pieces of advice I'd ever been given by him. I've lived a large life in my work and on the road and am prone to ebullience in my re-tellings, which largely fall on deaf ears. I asked him;

"How do you translate enormous experience to folks who ask 'Well, how was it?'"

He said;

"You say; 'It was fine' and for ninety-nine percent of the people that will suffice. For the rest you can elaborate."

***

Thai Lottery

"Hey, I made some hard-boiled eggs for you today."
"Oh, sorry, honey, cannot eat egg today."

"What, some mystical egg-free day on the Buddhist calendar?"

"No, but I play lottery today, and for Thai people is not lucky to eat something that look like number you play. I want 'zero' today, and egg look like zero."

"Yer kiddin' me?"

Afternoon.

"Honey, I just win 40,000 baht in lottery today. Now you believe?"

"Yer kiddin' me?"

***

Visakha Bucha Day

Visakha Bucha Day is one of the high holy days in Thailand for Buddhists, marking the birth, enlightenment and death of the Lord Buddha. It is mostly noted in the expat world for its strict clampdown on the sale of booze.

Several years ago I was tasked with showing an out-of-town friend a good time in Bangkok. It was unfortunate timing that he chose this day for his foray. He said;

"Man, this is your town, and I'll be sorely disappointed if you can't procure a beer for me."

They'd even cleared out the mini bars in the hotel rooms.

I was at wit's end, but he'd have none of it and unrelentingly persisted. Reaching deep into my bag of tricks I took him to a place I'd known about back in the day. One of the back-alley blow-job bars that used to litter the city. I walked up to the *mamasan* and asked for a couple of beers. She gave me a forlorn look and said;

"Very sorry but cannot. Is big Buddha day."

I said;

"I understand. Let me ask you though, you still serving blowjobs?"

She lit up and said;

"Oh, sure!"

"Then give us some dammed beers."

She laughed and said;

"OK, OK, but inside."

Happy Visakha Bucha day everyone.

***

Wrestling with demons

Stopped into a bar tonight. Quelle surprise.

Never one to waste an opportunity... I wound up befriending a trio of stupidly buffed special forces guys. There was an arm-wrestling table in the pub, and as one does, I challenged one of them to a duel. I put my lifetime of weight and savvy into it and felt extremely confident until my opponent said;

"OK, are you ready?"

"What do you mean; 'are you ready?' Aren't we already doing this?"

Four seconds later he smiled as I rubbed my loser's shoulder. And then to make matters worse, he performed the most honest yet humiliating gesture I've ever experienced - he complimented me on my moxie, shook my hand and gave me a 'brothers in arms' hug, which he performed as gingerly as if I were a hundred and thirty-year-old Fabergé egg.

Do not go gentle into that good night...

***

Mille Bornes

I spent several young, formative years in a foster home. My mom whose care I was legally in, was crazy and ill-equipped to care for a young child. My dad was a jet-setting playboy with a super model for a new wife and wanted nothing to do with a kid. So I was farmed out to an immigrant family for a few years who already had a few children of their own and enjoyed the extra income. They were French. The mother's name was Josette.

The one kinda sorta saving grace I suppose, for a young'un is that you have no frame of reference, (other than the world around you if you're at all perceptive) so the abnormal is just life. They played a French card game that I learned to love called *Mille Bornes*.

What I remember of it was that it was a car racing card game, and that if you were crafty, you could get these magic cards that would give you; unlimited gas, unlimited repairs, unlimited spare tires and, best of all, no speed limit. I think that has been the inspiration and metaphor for my life. Get all the no limit cards you can and win the game... as if...

***

Turned to Jelly

    Rough seas always remind me of a dive trip down south years ago. Everything was going swimmingly, as it were, when I noticed a giant jellyfish closing distance on me at an alarming rate. The faster I swam, the closer it got.
    In a panic I shot up to the surface and pitched myself onto the boat, breathlessly telling the dive master of my harrowing experience being chased by the jellyfish.
    The hardened 'seen it all' Aussie captain shook his head in dismay and said;
    "No eyes mate."
    "What's that?"
    "Jelly's ain't got no eyes mate. Can't have been chasing you."
    "But, but but..."
    "Give us yer gear, grab a beer and wait for the others. Yer secret's safe with me."

***

The Quick Read

    Watched a guy come into the little place I was having dinner and smiled with self-satisfaction at what a quick read he was for me.
    'Wife beater' t-shirt with a beer logo on it, a backwards sun visor, a shifty gaze, a couple of prison tattoos and clearly several outstanding warrants back in East L.A. for petty larceny and aggravated assault. By his side was an overly dolled up Thai gal who was doing a second-by-second assessment of her 'catch' and who had a business scheme to defraud as many foreigners as she could at the next full moon party.

And then his glass of red wine arrived, which he politely thanked his server for in a Dutch accent. He caught my gaze, tipped his glass in cheers and smiled, saying;

"So nice to have a decent meal after a year in the jungle working with hill-tribe people. This is one of the doctors at the AIDS clinic we work at. I thought she deserved a night out as well. Anyway, enjoy your meal."

***

Paging Mr. Ionesco

"Excuse me, but I just heard you order a coffee. Do you know that they have a promotion for coffee and a cake, and it's twenty baht cheaper than ordering a coffee by itself?"

"Really? No I didn't, but I don't really want any cake."

"But you don't need to eat it."

"That's true. Then I'll do that and just take the cake home. Thanks."

"OK, yeah, that's the catch. You can't take it home. It's only for their 'special' cake that must be eaten here."

"What are you talking about? It's ordered food. Of course I can take it home."

"No, it's their policy, so usually I just give it to the staff."

"OK then, excuse me, waiter, I'll have a coffee that I'll drink and a cake that I won't eat, for twenty baht less... Would you like my cake?"

"No, thank you, sir. I am full already."

"So anyway, where are you from?"

"San Francisco, I guess?"

"Really, I went to Davis."

"Oh, are you a veterinarian?"

"No, well almost, my wife was."

"Well I guess that makes me an almost dentist."

"Why, were you going to dental school?"
"No... my wife did."
"Yes, she was a good woman."
"Really, you knew her?"
"Who?"
"My wife?"
"No, I was talking about my wife."
"Yes, I figured..."
"What?"
"Excuse me, sir, manager decide to make exception for you. Can take cake you don't want to your home."
"Thank you so much, but I've decided to have my cake and eat it too."

***

Fair Trade

"Excuse me, sir, do you have a moment for a survey?"
"Sure."
"Have you bought any silk products while you were here?"
"No."
"Oh. Well thank you very much for your time."
"Awfully short survey. You work for a silk manufacturer?"
"No, actually I'm an engineering student in France but thought I'd get involved with an NGO while visiting my Khmer family here. We're trying to get an idea of people's feelings towards 'ethically based' wares."
"You mean like Fair Trade?"
"Yes, exactly."
"And what knowledge have you gleaned?"

"Honestly? I think I can speak freely with you, sir. Sadly nobody really gives a damn at any point of the commerce chain."

"Well then best of luck to you in engineering school."

***

Dateline: Sofia, 1992

I had a good friend who was a social worker at the county hospital in San Francisco. For some reason she had a Bulgarian paramour. The circumstances of how they'd met were never made clear to me, but it wasn't really my business.

One day I stopped in to chat with her between clients as was our infrequent routine. She asked where my next travels would be? I told her Eastern Europe. She asked if I would consider lecturing to a group of about thirty Bulgarian psychiatrists? I asked if she'd write off my trip.

The deal was set.

There are three things that I've always had an inordinate amount of fear about; quicksand, rabies shots, and public speaking.

I was due to lecture for three days. It seemed impossible. I wrote out my talk, interspersed as many humorous anecdotes as I could think of, and read what I'd written in front of a mirror. I read as slowly as if I had just learned English. It took forty-five minutes.

"No way it could be longer", I told her.

She told me to relax and that with translation, over-head image projection, technical failure, breaks, meals and questions, it would be more than enough. And sure as hell it was. Three days of lecturing at the Neuroscience Behavior Research Foundation of Sofia, Bulgaria.

Getting there was another matter.

I had a travel buddy in the U.S. military. He was a captain. He could fly anywhere he wanted to for free on a C-130 transport jet. I had to fly on a commercial plane like the rest of the world.

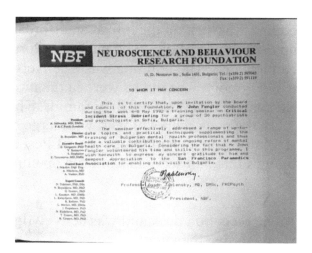

His only caveats were that he always had to have a set of his Class A 'whites' with him, a la *Officer and a Gentleman* and that he couldn't commit to a fixed arrival time as he was at the mercy of their schedule. He said that a three-day window was the best he could offer.

We agreed to meet in Budapest. He said that I should wait at the American Express office at three in the afternoon every day. I said;

"No way, buddy, we'll meet at the Gellert spa if it's gonna be anywhere!"

The Gellert is an ancient Roman bath house and hotel with thermal springs and topless Italian girls who seem to be perennially on 'Spring break'. And on day three, in the way these things usually pan out, he showed up.

I spent my time eating wild boar croquettes with pheasant soup, touring the Rococo style State Opera House and being battered around like a sock puppet by barrel chested men who were heaving soapy swatches of grape leaves at me. Such is the pulverizing experience of a rub down at the infamous Gellert spa.

My lodging was 'just up the hill' at an affordable youth hostel. Just up the hill turned out to be more of a formidable hike than I'd anticipated. The building was a converted seven-hundred-year-old armory. The bunks were in the turret rooms which still had cannon balls stacked in pyramids. The sides of the building bore the pock marks of war, with large chunks missing. Best of all it had a panoramic view of Pest through the narrowed windows that had served as muzzle openings for the cannons.

I got to the reception desk and was actively ignored by the bored and dismissive manager.
I said that I needed a bed. Without looking up from the newspaper he was so engrossed in, he muttered;
"Full, no bed."
We continued this little dance back and forth a few times until I grew weary and frustrated. It had been a long day. I went New York on him. I dropped my pack on the floor, slapped my hand on the counter and bore into his startled eyes and told him;
"I will stand here for the rest of my life until you have a bed!"
He gave the very slightest of smiles and said;
"Hokay ve have availability now."
It was four dollars for a room with four beds which lined the old track of the cannon emplacements. There were no other customers.

Non Compass Mentis

In the early nineties there were a few insurrections taking place in Eastern Europe as well as a few other hot spots in the world. Czechoslovakia was becoming two nations, and Yugoslavia was becoming something other worldly. They were all on the U.S. State Department's 'don't travel there' lists.

The Budapest train station didn't have the qualms, nor did they get the memo, so on day four we bought our tickets to Bulgaria.

At that time there were two possible overland routes to take. The first was the legal route through war torn Romania, which we were told; "yes is legal, but not recommend."

The second was through the officially off limits but "safer" Yugoslavia. So we boarded the train having splurged the extra thirty cents on a private compartment. The only other passengers in our car were a family of emphysemic gypsies.

A couple of hours passed which were filled with pleasant scenery and ox carts carrying babushkas who were swaddling babies atop piles of wheat.

We then crossed the Hungarian border into Yugoslavia when the train suddenly lurched to a stop. A double phalanx of double-time-marching, well-armed militia lined up on both sides of the train to prevent an escape from the compartment windows. They wore pristine uniforms and carried modern weapons and radios. They were in stark contrast to the day-to-day equipment that had been in circulation since the last war that was the common sight. This was not a good sign as these were spiffy and shiny new issues. They constituted a formidable and intimidating presence.

A group of about eight men boarded the train. My buddy and I were unperturbed as we assumed this was all a gypsy thang and nothing to do with two Americans traveling through a war-torn country without visas.

Sure enough we were ordered out of our compartment and a Kalashnikov was poked into my ribs.

That was followed by the bark of;
"Passport!"
We complied,
"VISA!!"
I gave a weak smile and the hopelessly stupid response of;
"Um... Mastercard?"
Curiously enough this did not endear us to them. That led to the inevitable;
"Vell, vell, vat's in zese packs?"
'Oh ya mean on top of the class 'A' captain's uniform? Well my friend's a bit anal and decided to photocopy all the Eastern European train schedules. Oh and those... well we sometimes like to look at birds with those high-powered miniature spy glasses.'
Shit, I wouldn't have believed us.
'Um, no blindfold, thanks.'
We were then summarily rousted off the train at gunpoint, much to the surprise and relief of the emphysemic gypsies.
We were escorted into adjoining jail cells inside the train station. My indignant pal starting up with the first of his many;
"Do you know who I am?" statements, which were followed by impressive sounding initials. He increased his tirade with;
"Hey, we're Americans, damn it!", and
"I'm with the Army!", to which I acidly shot back;
"Hey, shut the fuck up, man! Maybe those aren't all good things to be right now."
We'd been friends for years and I'd never seen him flap. To me he was unflappable.
That was until the desk sergeant came in. He was wearing an old woolen fatigue coat and from his pockets he pulled out two plump and calloused civil servant's hands. This was a land of cold war central casting characters, and he was no exception.

He was large and menacing but held a measured calm. He appeared war weary but was brimming with alertness and had quick eyes. He landed heavily in his chair which creaked and popped as he dropped into it.

There was a large book on his desk like the kind that hold title deeds in land Assessor's offices. He began methodically paging through the lines as he slid our passports down an endless list of personae non grata, slowing at my buddy's name and pointedly sounding out; "oh, L-e-v-i-n-s-k-i?!"

My friend could have played lead on one of the *Twilight Saga* adventures right then. I don't know where all the blood in his face drained to, but it was sudden and profound. He meekly turned towards me and through the bars of our adjacent cells stammered;

"Hey, what if they don't like Jews here?"

I said;

"Hello! Now will you shut the fuck up? We're not in an ideal spot if you hadn't noticed. How much dough you got on you anyway? Not that they couldn't just clean out our pockets themselves I guess."

It was a very long few hours. Through the bars of the window to the outside we noticed that our train had been held the whole time. It was approaching dusk. I imagined the weary desk sergeant weighing out his options of ending his day mopping up a nice plate of goulash with some moist doughy bread and a glass of Raki, or dealing with a mountain of paperwork and an unappreciative one-star general who would have to drive all the way in from Belgrade.

He seemed to decide suddenly as he slid open a desk drawer, pulled out a long black handled stamp, and slammed it noisily into our passports. He jutted his chin to the gate keeper, thrust the papers towards us, and in a wonderfully minimal Slavic tone said;

"GO!"

Back on the train without even having to pay a bribe, our abandoned packs, while having been rifled through, were intact. We then did the only thing possible after an experience like that, we found the liquor cart.

Bulgaria is the world's source for rose attar. Ninety percent of the rose essence that's used in air fresheners, greeting cards and cheap perfume comes from the Valley of the Roses. What they don't turn into romantic fodder goes into liquor. This was a cart full of miniature 'airplane' bottles of the stuff. It wasn't particularly tasty but was numbing and sleep inducing which was the desired effect. We awoke in Sofia with a scene that would have made Gulliver proud. Two grown men splayed out on benches and covered with tiny empty bottles.

My favorite part of lecturing there was that about half of the participants spoke English and would immediately laugh at my jokes.
The other half had to wait for the translator, and I would be treated to a seven second delay of laughs from them. One of the participants was a man named Luchezar Hranov. He ran the panic disorder clinic at the psychiatric hospital. He was a bear; a huge thoughtful and passionate intellectual. We bonded immediately and he invited me out to his apartment the first evening to meet with a group of his colleagues for "further discussion".
There would be no labels on the vodka bottles.

A taxi out to block 92, section 48, building 6, room 104 was only distinguished from all the others by its red light which barely illuminated the otherwise gray world of this Soviet tenement.
Trying to gear myself up for the scrutiny that a foreign guest would engender, under the playfully watchful eyes of post-Soviet era shrinks, I added my own bottle to the mix of those that were already in full service on the dining room table.

The topics were deep and the vibe playful. Hoping to ingratiate myself to the group I grabbed one of the unlabeled bottles of vodka and leaned towards the glass with the most diminished level of fluid.

My new friend interrupted his own soliloquy and turned towards me. He slammed his bear paw flat onto the table and boomed in a belligerent tone;

"Zis is typical American reaction! You people -you have no idea vat it is to go viz nothing! You can't imagine an empty glass. You only know excess. In Bulgaria ve don't refill the glass until it is empty. Ve know empty!!"

And then his playful smile returned, but his eyes betrayed a lingering scorn.

"By ze vay my friend, vhen you return to your country, vould you be so kind as to send me some two-ply?"

"I'm sorry, what was that?" I asked.

"In Bulgaria ve cannot get ze two ply, you know for take ze shit. Ah yes, two ply, zis is what your country is good at. Very soft. Very decadent."

Then there was the exit strategy. Safely ensconced in the relatively Euro friendly womb of Bulgaria, we had to figure a way out. Train? Don't think so.

So I stumbled upon an airline called; Bulgarian Lucky Flights.

'Well do ya, punk?'

The U.S. makes shiny new jetliners which they fly for five to ten years. Showing some signs of wear they sell them to places like Mexico who in turn run them down a bit before offloading them to places like Turkey, who then ensure that nothing whatsoever is in working order before giving them to Bulgaria.

The good thing about marginalized economies, from an end user's perspective, is that there is no labor premium.

Workers are poorly paid, and anything mechanized, or factory produced, is necessarily more expensive. To wit, Bulgarian Lucky Flights employed babushkas to cook their in-flight meals.

A long line of heavy set, kerchief wearing, gulag shuffling old women brought tray after tray of hot home cooked dumplings and goulash for the passengers. To date it was the best in-flight meal of my life.

And then to our great surprise the plane left the ground, and back into the ersatz 'West' we flew.

Dateline: Prague!

***

Someday my prints will come

Going out to my patio, that I'd abandoned the previous night when the monsoon rains arrived, I spotted some animal prints on a cushion that'd been left out. They were undoubtably put there by some water-logged creature seeking shelter. It made me think of my first-time tracking footprints long ago.

When I first moved to the California Sierras, it was the equivalent of going to the moon for this city boy. I made friends with an ole' codger who'd lived there for eternity. I asked about the ins 'n outs of getting things repaired, as this was a physically isolated area, and you were a hundred bucks into travel time even before they got to you. I said;

"Who do you call around here to get things fixed?"

He looked at me a little confused and said;

"What do ya mean 'who do ya call?', ya don't call nobody, ya fix it yerself."

I tried to clarify with;

"No, I mean real stuff, like a water heater or something."

"Ya fix that too!"

I conceded that my lofty education hadn't provided me with any practical life skills whatsoever. He looked me up and down and smirked, saying;
"Don't worry, I'll learn ya."
And so he did.

One of the first things I did with my newfound mountain exuberance there, was to buy a tracking guide to explore my 'estate'. I'd bought ninety acres of rural mountain land, surrounded on three sides by national forest, so I essentially owned a million acres.

I had two year-round streams, some remnants of old prospectors' shacks, a wooden Petticoat Junction-esque water tower and an ancient 'wagon trail' that bisected it all.

Per the giant title deed book that denoted the parameters of ownership, I was in perpetuity required to maintain a fourteen-foot-wide wagon trail. I asked the realtor how one would go about complying with an archaic and obsolete demand on land that was originally won in a poker game. He said he had no idea, but to;
"Just consider it maintained".

The first day out my face was glued to the ground, looking for signs of bear, mountain lion, fox, bobcat and sasquatch - all of which had been recently sighted.

I was thrilled then to come across a set of fresh and exotic prints right next to the stream where I'd decided to keep my beer chilled. I whipped out my trusty guide and excitedly leafed through all the possible matches, until getting to my 'aha!' moment and then reading *'canis familiaris'*.

I was ecstatic until turning the page and seeing the accompanying photo of a domestic house dog.

And then, to my complete embarrassment, I looked up into the sweet pleading eyes of my very own pooch who had undoubtedly just placed those prints there.

***

John Fengler

Imagine

"Paint the 'cyc'", I was told. This after spending three hours, from 6 a.m. onward, tediously plumbing the depths of dozens of boxes of Total cereal in search of enough 'perfect' flakes to fill a bowl. And subsequently being dismissed with;

"Shit, we're only shooting the top of the bowl, man. Nobody's gonna see what's under there."

A 'cyc' is the film industry's slang for a cyclorama. It's basically a curved wall that forms the foundation, the backdrop of any film set or theatre production. It was developed in Germany in the nineteenth century as a means of creating the illusion of infinity and often has a distant sky or horizon painted on it. The harsh lights and changing needs of the shoot dictate that it be painted over with each new production. This task invariably falls to the lowliest of staff, the production assistant.

I filled the rest of my morning mindlessly rolling off white paint onto the infinity wall, oftentimes losing myself in the curve and its illusory feel. Not an unpleasant way to pass the workday. Next was the shopping list and most importantly the petty cash. I was to get all manner of greasy, oily, stain-inducing foods, including cakes, ice creams and sauces. This was after all, going to be a commercial for Stain Master carpet.

The set was built, the carpet unfurled, the 'housewife' was made up and clothed. The lights were set, the cameraman was in position, the prop master was in place.

"Ready... .and Action! Cue the cake drop!"

It is by now early evening and looks to be a long shoot. The problem was the central character of this commercial, the unstainable Stain Master carpet wasn't living up to its claim. Even in the illusory photo and lighting manipulated world of a film set the stuff was just crap.

But at $60,000 for the cost of that day's production we were destined for take after take. And those were 1980 dollars. December 8, 1980 dollars to be exact.

The day looked to be interminable, with the lowly assistant staff already approaching eighteen hours on the set, when out of the blue, at about 10:45 at night, the director shouted in exasperation;

"Aw, Fuck it. Cut. Wrap. Everybody go home!"

I didn't need to be told twice, nor did I need to be noticed in case there was anything else that needed to be done that nobody else wanted to do. So I slipped out the side door of the set and hailed a cab.

"70th and Columbus".

We were coming from the Lower East side, so the driver shot through the park and up Central Park West. A quick drive which normally doesn't even leave me enough time to imagine myself collapsing exhaustedly into bed. But;

Shit, a traffic jam and at this time of night? God damn it! Another stupid NY spectacle impeding my progress home. Oh, fuck it.

"I'll just get out here and hoof it past the crowds at the Dakota. Thanks."

The Dakota is a legendary and seminal landmark to the NYC skyline. Built in the late nineteenth century, it has a gothic presence, made no less imposing by having served as the set location for one of the creepiest movies ever made; Rosemary's Baby. It was also more exaltedly known as the residence of John and Yoko. Tired and disgusted I couldn't help but be drawn into the rubbernecker's wonderland of late-night crowds, NY streets, and the 'wow they're actually drawing a chalk outline for some poor fucker, just like in the movies.' OK I'll bite...

"Hey what's going on?"

And through a wail of tears, a woman turned to me and said;

"Oh my God. It's John Lennon. He's been shot!"

John and Yoko were local fixtures who famously had their NY digs in the Dakota. There was a deeply intuited respect for the couple's privacy that the locals strictly adhered to. It was a tacit agreement that they got to wander the neighborhood un-molested and 'un-recognized' and we got to soak in the thrill and joy of going to the supermarket and turning to our friends or lovers and saying;

"Hey don't look, but... I said don't look... but you see that woman holding up that cantaloupe? That's Yoko... and John."

It was a searing dagger of loss, the feeling of which has not lessened over the years.

It was compounded by the realization that I had cursed his demise, selfishly, unknowingly, as just another impediment to my slumber. An icon of my youth, a protected if un-met friend and a beacon of hope and inspiration, was now lined with chalk on a cold sidewalk on the Upper West Side.

And still through the sorrow and the incomprehension, excited whispers could be overheard.

"Hey, isn't that Woody and Mia looking out the window?"

And then as the crowds eventually thinned and only the chalk outline remained, the shock, which reverberates to this day, sends a deep chill up my spine. And whenever I cross the threshold of his death while strolling past the Dakota, or stranger yet, in the way that time and events conflate, I can't look at a deep pile white shag carpet without silently singing; Imagine.

***

Jaffna bus

A couple of years ago I took a trip to Jaffna, in the very north of Sri Lanka on a train line that had been shut due to civil war for twenty-five years. Old school traveling it was. Comfortable it was not.

"Excuse me, someone told me you have an air-conditioned bus to Colombo from here?"

"Yes, sir, a very nice bus. It leaves from this place one time per day and is very comfortable."

"Wow, comfortable, I can't imagine.
Can you sell me a ticket now please?"

"Oh yes, sir. One ticket only then?"

"Yes, Great. What time does it leave?"

"Oh bus is broken, sir, it will not be going anywhere."

"But, but, but... OK let me have a ticket on the overcrowded, overheated and overly loud bus then, please."

"Roadblock."

"I'm sorry?"

"No busses leaving here today. Having roadblock, sir".

"But, but, but"

***

Caen

I made Herb's column several times. A great source of pride I must admit. I still miss him! A couple of my faves from about '95 I believe.

Macabre humor department:

John M. Fengler made a startling discovery in the Neptune Society's Columbarium, off Geary Blvd., wherein repose the ashes of some of our most distinguished citizens. It's a sign on the third floor, undergoing repairs, which reads "Pardon Our Dust" . . .

After the arrest of Gary Busey for a cocaine overdose, S.F. paramedic John Fengler was heard to wonder,
"Say, just what is a proper dose of cocaine, anyway?"

***

Gout

A surgeon pal of mine once said;
"The role of the physician is to have his or her treatment correspond to the patient's own spontaneous recovery."
As a dedicated sybarite there is no one in the world who deserves to suffer from gout more than I do. If you can't do the time, don't do the crime, the saying goes. Be that as it may, it is quite debilitating, for reasons not the least of which is that it garners so little sympathy.
"Oh your toe hurts?"
"No, fuck you, I'll kill you if you even look at it! That's how much it hurts."
Or more eloquently in the words of the eighteenth-century writer Lady Mary Wortley Montagu;
"People wish their enemies dead – but I do not; I say give them the gout."
My empathetic girlfriend came home with an armful of herbs and plants and proceeded to concoct a "double double toil and trouble... eye of newt and toe of frog" witch's brew, to replace the traditional pharmaceuticals I've been taking to little effect.
In the 'hard to prove a negative' vein, I am happy to report that I'm a pain free convert.
Let the games resume.

***

Luck of the 'Oirish

A couple of years ago I celebrated St. Patrick's Day at the UN Irish pub in Chiang Mai, as I do most years now. Several pints in; the gal with the accordion had the crowd whipped into a foot stompin' frenzy.

At the crescendo of one tune she yelled out, "OK, who here's Oirish?"

A roar from every corner of the room erupted.

She then yelled;

"Not you wanker Americans, REAL Oirish?"

You could've heard a pin drop.

In 2009 I found myself in Montevideo, Uruguay on St. Patrick's Day. Globetrotting can be a lonely thing sometimes, especially on holidays. I thought;

'Shit there's an Irish pub everywhere. Why not here?!' And then I found The Shannon.

It was four in the afternoon. There was one lone picnic table set up outside with four other travelers already encamped; two young bucks from Liverpool, a lad from Aberdeen in Scotland and a jig dancin' lass from Dublin. I asked to join them. They of course welcomed me open arms while one said;

"Ah American - we'll see how long ya last, mate."

Five thousand people had packed into the square around where we had pitched up fifteen hours earlier.

That was the last time in my adult life I remember seeing the sun rise without me having set a wake-up alarm at home. I love a good challenge.

They say, 'everyone's Irish on March 17th'. Happy St. Patrick's Day everyone.

***

Kep

Kep has one pool table.

It's a surprisingly good one, with minimal roll considering it's constantly being re-shimmed to account for the fluctuations from heat expansion, general warp of the floorboards and saturation from the tidal splash just beneath it.

The regular crowd shuffles in and consists of mercenaries, journalists, generic outlaws, NGO workers and tourists. Conversations tend to stay light and predictable, with a degree less of the usual wariness one finds with this mix. I think it's far enough off the grid that everyone gets cred just for being there.

Soki is charming as the multilingual proprietor. Her story told a thousand times over; romance, funding of a 'dream bar' and eventual abandonment. There's a hopeful resignation on her face.

Kim - a French accented Khmer man, kicks off his flip flops and says, sportingly;

'We play for drinks, OK?!'

I let him know that my marriages were the extent of my gambling career. He laughed while throwing his head back and then conceded to play just for fun. I beat him handily... at first.

Going for a refill I'm stopped by a Canadian, who while holding his watch, is asking the 16-year-old Khmer farm girl behind the bar, if they use daylight savings time here? He'd have better luck asking about the tooth fairy, than to try and explain a concept like that here.

A small group enters and takes up residence in a far corner of this open-air bar. She is dressed in haute couture beachwear, he with designer sunglasses. In tow are half a dozen Khmer kids all holding fruit smoothies. The couple sees me, and both give a knowing smile that says, I see them and won't bother them.

I think they are Brad and Angelina, but soon am disabused of that thought. They are something akin to that though.

Walking back the kilometer or so to my bungalow, on wide and exceedingly unlit jungle lined streets, I catch occasional movements from the stands of saw brush and banana palms. A brief shudder before the calm settles back in and I remember that it was the Rambo movie I was recalling, which was on the reception office's TV earlier today, rather than any real threat.

It's remarkably peaceful. I doubt I'd try the same stroll at night in Detroit.

A former hang out for the Khmer and French elite, this little town now is the destination of choice for Phnom Penh locals on weekend retreats, to fill up on as many fresh crab as they can eat. Come Sunday night and for the rest of the week, it is a ghost town; gloriously so.

In many ways it could be any sleepy fishing village in; Belize, Marseille or Molokai. But it's not. It's Asia.

***

Sometimes people inadvertently speak the truth

"You're a good guy, John. You're the best out of all these losers here."
???
"No, no I meant..."

***

Ladle

I spent 3 minutes staring at a bird on my ledge, its head tucked under its wing, raindrops glinting off the newly returned sun rays. Its tail dipped down into the utensil tray on which it was perched.

I experienced a great calm during those 3 minutes. And then the lighting changed, and I realized it had been a ladle all along.

Paging Dr. Kafka.

***

Steel Wheels

One of my 'brushes with greatness', was backstage at the Stones; 1989 Steel Wheels tour, Day on the Green, Oakland, California.

I ran into a couple of friends from college.

My friend's wife had a backstage pass on her shirt which my eyes were transfixed upon. She looked at me and said;
"John, why are you staring at my boobs?"
I said;
"What? No, I've seen yer boobs. I'm looking at your pass!"
She said;
"Oh, that? You want it?"
She then peeled it off and slapped it on my chest.
I said;
"Just so there's no misunderstandings... you do know what this is right??"
"Yeah, I don't care."
You know where the Road Runner shoots off and leaves a ghost outline of his form? That's what I left. It was, as you'd expect, awesome. What they don't tell you, is that there's a backstage pass and then there's an impenetrable 'Mick' pass, where the actual band members are. But all things being equal, rock on. Thrill of a lifetime. RIP Charlie.

***

Probing Phnom Penh

A Royce rolls by indignantly blaring its horn, demanding quarter in a clot of Sisowath Quay funeral processions. It swerves past a beggar boy who has no quarter to offer. The Sisyphean dance macabre continues as old ladies squat in blood, scraping the scales of injustice off two-dollar fish that will transform into haute cuisine at five-star restaurants later today, unless they go unsold and become yesterday's stew.

A school bell rings and startles a girl from atop of a pile of garbage.

Her uniform of gray and sores and resignation, starched and cleansed of hope, glistens off the tin cans she is collecting.

The carcasses of petrodollar investments crane into the sky. The legions of former workers awaiting the next boom in trade, while away the day with a dog-eared deck of cards and some local brew. The lavender scented liberals tipping gin, infused with pride by the dent they've made with their NGOs line the riverfront.

The monsoon rains will wash this all away again soon. The issues and the bar girls will be skirted. Wallets and lemons will be squeezed. It happens every year, brother.

***

Things I still love about Phnom Penh

No matter how irretrievably lost you get, you're never more than a $1 motorbike ride from salvation.

Warm French bread served with even warmer Khmer smiles. A cool Mekong breeze and hot American jazz.

It is a Phoenix rising; with an unflinching sense of its recent past, but resolutely embracing the future.

Cell phone calls are virtually free.

Being a 'brother', as in 'thank you brother for giving me job today'.

A round of drinks for the girls; $8

It has a great airport!

A repository for extraordinary people. Chatting with a shorts clad man from New Delhi wearing an Australian bush hat and a goofy smile.

"So here on holiday?"

"Oh no my friend, I am having a consulting firm with the World Bank."

Bee-hive hairdos

Chaos theory.

Sitting in a rattan chair drinking a glass of wine on the riverfront in Phnom Penh. Three completely naked children are standing just outside the reach of the awning, drenched in monsoon madness, their mom making the universal begging gesture of puckered fingers to mouth. They furtively glance inside at the staff. They know their place. It's all so understood.

It would be an astonishing photo in a land rich with poverty. But it would be considered child porn by some. By many. Street porn it is. A centerfold.
I have now been in and around these parts for 32 years, and in many ways, it still feels like day 1. In many ways it is.
'You cannot step into the same river twice.'
Last night at "Phnom Penh's newest exciting and metropolitan alleyway bar"
The regular crowd shuffles in. A UN de-mining team out of Adelaide, who reassuringly said;
"Oh Battambang? Yeah, just stay on the main road mate and ya should be fine";
A Chinese engineer who only spoke Swedish, a portly Englishman smoking a footlong Cuban cigar, three well turned-out gals from the US embassy with that universally contemptuous look of; 'shit if we had been posted anywhere else, guys would actually be hitting on us', a chef from the Four Seasons Tanzania and a quartet of French male models wearing mostly unbuttoned white shirts and Cheshire cat grins. Now back of a van on a 6-hour terror ride through the Cambodian countryside - which amazingly enough offers free wi-fi.
'Huh what's a herd of water buffalo doing on the road? Oh I see we're not on the road...oh there we go, back on."
I hired a driver for the day while visiting Battambang in the Northwest of Cambodia.
It is home to some of the most well preserved French colonial architecture in the Kingdom but also to some of the darkest periods of Khmer Rouge oppression in the land.

My driver inevitably brought me and I'm sure every white face he could find, to the home of a woman who had a burgeoning winery. It was in all senses a tourist trap in the middle of nowhere. I politely tasted all their products and trying to ingratiate myself to the host, announced one wine to be 'delicious' in Khmer.

The owner feigned being impressed at my language skills and asked how I could speak Khmer and whether I'd ever been to her country before?

I said that yes, a long time ago I worked in a refugee camp that was not all that far from the nearby Thai border. Her demeanor immediately changed, and a reflective cloud and a reverential pall crossed her face. She snapped something to the kitchen staff who whisked away our tourist samples leaving the table clean. Always a dicey bet owning up to any prior relationship in currently land-mined areas and to peoples with shattered histories no matter one's 'innocence', as those values are ascertained by the hosts.

This woman looked at me solemnly, and with a slight smile and the smallest of head bows said;

"You are a friend of my family. Now we will have lunch and 'the good wine'."

***

Trout Fishing in San Francisco

I made friends with local photographer Erik Weber some years ago up in the Sierras. I found out he had a close friendship with Richard Brautigan. When Erik saw my eyes light up, he said;

"Well, I have some shots available if you're interested."

I was very interested and unearthed a photo in a friend's basement where I store my few remaining sentimental items.

    I stalked Richard Brautigan. Every day for two years, in the late 70s, I'd go and sit at Enrico's on Broadway, as I'd heard it was one of his favorite haunts in North Beach. No idea what I'd even say to my poet icon if I actually met him but patiently wait, I did.

    And lo and behold he showed up one day. What I hadn't counted upon was that he'd be surrounded by an impenetrable circle of beautiful women and acolytes of every stripe. I sat forlorn over my cappuccino until destiny struck. A moment came, as they do, when he needed to relieve himself.

Coincidentally, so did I.

A lifetime of fandom since high school, just one urinal away. Not normally the best time to start a conversation with a stranger, and this was no exception. I made several false starts, looking his way and cocking my head to offer a quip, desperately searching for the best quote of his, the best opening line to prove my fealty to his works.

He of course gave me the universal 'get away from me creep' look, zipped up and went back to his table. Not a word between us, but I was satisfied at least in knowing that our interaction, no matter how humiliating for me, was exactly the kind of thing he would have written about. Enrico's Cafe and Richard Brautigan…

Sigh. I do love my city.

***

The Ecdysiast

"Hey, you seem nice. I need a new sex partner. Are you interested?"

I spit out the mouthful of toothpaste.

I looked up into the face of a young woman that was gazing into the communal bathroom mirror of the Ryokan, the Japanese guest house that we were both apparently staying in. I said;

"I'm sorry, can you repeat that?"

She told me that her current partner suddenly split and that there was an immediate opening for her stage act up on the Ginza, the infamous gentleman's club district in Tokyo.

"I'll pay you fifteen thousand U.S. for six weeks. We'd have five shows a night."

Weighing out all the implications of this startling offer, including the fact that I was poor, twenty-five, horny and that she was an attractive gal to boot, I ended up with;
"Ya know I just don't think I could do that."
She was facing herself in the mirror now, her tongue partially extended as she stroked mascara onto her lash. She said;
"Oh don't worry, you get used to it."
I shyly reiterated that I didn't think I could 'DO' that!
"Ya know... five shows a night?!"
She paused for a moment, churning my response over and then laughed, saying;
"Oh man, ya don't come! It's just a show for the Japanese businessmen."
I wished her good luck, but regretfully declined. To this day I regret I declined.

Was in a club in the Roppongi district in Tokyo, I think. Might have been the Lexington Queen circa 1982. Sting was there, surrounded by an impenetrable coterie of young things. Never did get to say; 'hey'.
I was seated alone in the catbird booth. Lucky I am that way. My waiter arrived with a very serious pinstripe suited contingent of Japanese 'businessmen' behind him. He asked if I would mind moving to another table.
Arrogant New Yorker newbie that I was, I said;
"No way, pal. I was here first."
He gave me an imploring look that I carry with me to this day and said;
"I recommend that you move."
"… I understand."

Still green as a stick, I went into a public bath shortly thereafter, naked except for holding a washcloth over my nuts, as they do. There were three ancient men in one tub and a sumo-sized guy in another.

The sumo-sized guy had the most wild and elaborate tattoos I'd ever seen. He also had only three fingers on his right hand. Stupid innocent fuck that I am, I immediately headed over to him.

The three old guys went bug-eyed and gave me a 'No, no don't go there' look. The sumo guy caught their look and gave me a huge smile and beckoned me into his tub.

My second brush with death with the Yakuza.

Ironically, I would wind up on-stage years later during a sex act, with Japanese businessmen enthusiastically looking on. We were called for the;

"Fall at 240 O'Farrell St. Please use the side entrance. No further details."

It is with the greatest of Zen detachments that the good medic approaches a call. There are many reasons someone could fall and many distances for them to fall from. It could be from a bar stool after misjudging the floor, or a bridge after misjudging their station in life, or a collapse from a missed beat in their heart after misjudging the effects of decades of neglect, if it was even a fall at all.

I remember during my upstart days, which were filled with wonder, protocols, terror and algorithms. We received a dispatch over a scratchy radio for the "O.D".

Great, this I was good at. It was a good six minutes away, even with lights and sirens and I was ready for whatever drug induced event this was. I knew my overdose algorithms. I had my narcotic antagonist for the heroin call, my Atropine dosages for the organophosphate exposure, D50 for the insulin O.D., Valium, Verapamil, Glucagon, sodium bicarb and even a vial of amyl nitrate for the obscure possibility of a cyanide ingestion. I had my pharmacology down.

It was with great surprise then, pulling up on the scene and jumping out of the ambulance with a syringe in each hand, to find a teenage Latina laying on the front lawn with her legs spread and her mother screaming at us in Spanish while cradling the gooey face of an infant that was making its debut from the young girls' loins.

"No, sorry guys", our dispatcher said, "it was for the OB, not the O.D."

This was in my pre-Zen days as an intern. You are given a leash by your preceptors while in training, but these are real events with real patients, occurring in real time. A hesitation results in a snap of that leash. I froze. I couldn't come around to the actual nature of the call and they knew it.

I was mentally locked into what I had expected it to be. My preceptors pushed past me to deliver the child and to attend to the post-delivery needs of the teen mother, as well as attempting to calm the hysteria of the teen's mother. I went back to lick my wounds. And so it was, with this developed Zen approach to my job, did I enter the side entrance of 240 O'Farrell St. for the fall.

The side door opened directly onto a stage that was drenched in green and pink light. Sultry strip music was playing overhead, and a ridiculously large breasted woman lay unconscious on the stage floor. A sea of Japanese businessmen sat beaming in the front two rows, the trench coats on their laps flapping wildly, their smiles broadening at the 'ambulance skit' that was unfolding for them.

I caught sight of a scruffy miscreant on the side of the stage who I accurately assessed to be the manager. I barked at him to turn the house lights on and to;

"Clear those guys out!"

The Fellini-esque scene revealed itself to not be a fall at all but a cardiac arrest that had occurred during a particularly vigorous moment of our ecdysiast's performance, where she had been probing her loins with a giant phallus.

We are trained to leave 'impaled' objects in place, lest we disturb something going on inside that we cannot see. So it was, with a large dildo protruding from between this stripper's legs did we then attempt to revive her heart. She was the headliner it turned out.

Her fame and notoriety were in part the result of the amount of implant she had in her breasts. She was celebrated not only for their disproportionate size but also for her mettle in the courts where she had successfully persuaded the judge to allow her to write off her surgery as a job-related tax deduction.

CPR is generally the first step in any attempted resuscitation, where hands are placed flat on the chest for compressions. The problem was that her décolletage did not allow for any such hand placement. The best we could do was to make a vertical approach on the wall of Everest and hope that we could displace enough of her chest to stimulate her heart.

Next up was the placement of defibrillator paddles, which also had us placing them at opposing vertical angles. She was at this point flatline, that is without pulse or any sign of cardiac activity. We charged the paddles, shouted "CLEAR" and depressed the switch.

Her body jumped from the shock, which forcefully ejected her pelvic lodger and sent it skittering off the stage. But more importantly it jump-started her heart into a viable rhythm. She was unfortunately pronounced dead sometime later at the hospital.

I was told that refunds were not given at the strip club.

Days tend to run in themes. It's one of the idiosyncratic truths to the profession. Start the day with a freeway crash and it was gonna be a trauma day for sure. A left over drunk in a doorway from the night before meant another twelve hours of homeless calls. And a lunchtime cardiac arrest in a strip club meant off to the 'happy clap' church, "CPR in progress".

My association with the church has been limited to the 'must visits' of foreign travels, and the occasional wedding, funeral service or concert, as they are famous for in places like Paris, where the acoustics are brilliant. And of course they have been the inevitable locale for job related medical events.

For those I am a true pantheist, be it Anton Lavey's Church of Satan for the 'accidental' stabbing, or Grace Cathedral for the tumble off the alter.

By far the most enthusiastic and beguiling of the bunch are the black American Baptist churches, not to be confused with the fire and brimstone, damn you to hell attitude of the white Southern Baptist churches. The black ones are lovingly referred to as 'happy clap' churches, due to their vigorous and positive celebration of life, as well as death, through song and dance laced sermons, prayer and, of course, their clapping.

It was on this cardiac arrest themed day that we were dispatched out to the Bayview Tabernacle Baptist Church for the "resuscitation in progress". We were politely and professionally escorted into the middle of the congregation where we found an eighty-three-year-old woman, dressed in her Sunday best, who we were informed had;

"Gotten the vapors. She just done lay down right here, and Lordy I think her soul just done passed right from her."

While mass continued around us, we placed cardiac monitor leads on her chest, as a group of satin robed women from the choir closed ranks around us, blotting out much of the available light.

I assumed they were there to preserve our patient's modesty, but they asked if they could pray while we worked? I said; "sure", assuming it would be silent prayer.

Wrong.

They proceeded to launch into song with ebullient voices. We continued our interventions, checking for this and ruling out that.

At one point I checked her blood sugar and ascertained that her glucose levels were dangerously low, enough to render her in this seemingly dead state. I winked at my partner, asked him for a vial of Glucagon, which is a drug that releases and transiently raises the blood glucose levels from the pancreas.

Its effects are sudden and dramatic. I held the vial at the IV tip and looked up to the choir that was now singing in earnest and somberly said;

"All right I need you to give it everything you've got!" and then depressed the plunger. Moments later our patient's eyelids sprang open, and the choir women began reeling around with;

"Lordy, Lordy, Lordy, oh Jesus, thank ya Lord for bringin' these miracle workers to be with us today."

The entire congregation then gathered around to witness this resurrection, and our noses were filled with the strong smell of gardenias that were stuck in the hats and bosoms of the elderly women that were pressing in to join with us.

We loaded our, now back to life, patient up and departed with smiles all around, safe in the knowledge that we had at least another hour until we would be dispatched to our next miracle.

**

John Fengler
Phnom Penh
September 2023

Sightings

That's Fengler, if I'm not mistaken.

Panama hat and cigarillo; goatee, from disguises 101.

He's flourishing a wine list, and he's polishing an apercu.

Is he just pleased to see us, or is he carrying a gun?

I'll be damned if that's not Fengler, doing absinthe in the bar,

Yes, I could swear it was Fengler glad-handing bar girls or photographing hors d'oeuvres,

And wasn't that Fengler jumping on Mekong boats and sharing his travel notes while strumming a guitar?

I thought I saw Fengler, but I could have been wrong, at a juke-joint in Langley spinning Johnny Cash songs.

Hey, wasn't that Fengler with the chick and the cool, mastering hit and myth, and telling it old-school?

Yes, that was most likely Fengler.

Fengler, our louche raconteur, checking into the Lux and dispensing the lore.

Yes, I think that was probably Fengler.

Yes, I think that was Fengler, for sure.

John Gartland

The Poet Noir

John Fengler

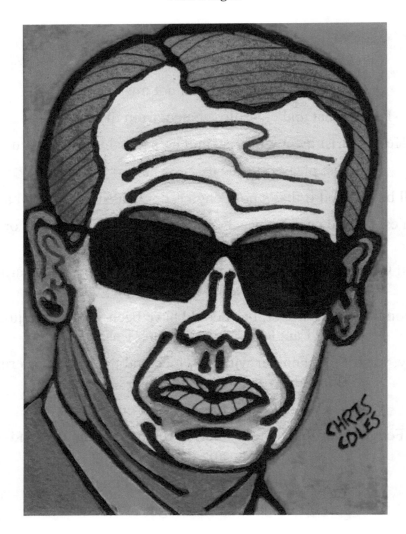

This painting of John Fengler, by Chris Coles, hung on the wall of Check Inn 99 in Bangkok for many years. Like the image that appears on page 202, it is reproduced here with the artist's permission.

***

Made in United States
Troutdale, OR
11/22/2023

14821555R00156